The PUBERTY Book

Wendy Darvill and Kelsey Powell

SIXTH EDITION

Gill Books
Hume Avenue
Park West
Dublin 12
www.gillbooks.ie

Gill Books is an imprint of M.H. Gill and Co.

This edition was first published in Australia and New Zealand in 2016
as *The Puberty Book* (Sixth Edition) by Hachette Australia
(an imprint of Hachette Australia Pty Limited), and this Gill Books
edition is published by arrangement with Hachette Australia Pty Ltd.

978 07171 8326 5

Print origination by O'K Graphic Design, Dublin

Printed by ScandBook, Sweden
This book is typeset in 12/16 pt Sabon Lt Sd.

A CIP catalogue record for this book is available from the British
Library.

5 4 3 2 1

Contents

Foreword

This sixth edition of *The Puberty Book* provides up-to-date information for young people growing up in today's society. More than ever before, young people have access to information from the internet, television and magazines. They are also communicating more and more through texts and social media. This sixth edition includes information on the issues arising from new technologies and offers strategies on how to use them safely. It also provides discussion about some of the social issues facing young people today.

To help young people develop healthy and positive attitudes to growing up and sexuality, it is important that they receive information that is accurate and easy to understand. Young people also need to be equipped with the confidence and skills to navigate through the abundance of information and messages they receive, some of it accurate, some of it not.

Despite the vast new sources of information available, it is through example and communication that parents and carers play the most significant role in providing a child's sexuality education. This new edition of *The Puberty Book* will help young people and their parents and carers to build on their knowledge, reduce anxieties, dispel some myths and correct misinformation.

Kelsey Powell

Acknowledgements

I would like to thank those who assisted with the publication of the sixth edition of *The Puberty Book*. As always, thank you to the educators at True (formerly Family Planning Queensland) who are always so generous in sharing their knowledge and experiences of working with young people.

I am also grateful to the team at Hachette Australia who have provided support and encouragement since *The Puberty Book* was first published in 1995.

Kelsey Powell

Introduction

This book is about puberty. Puberty is the process of changing from a child to an adult and is caused by the release of hormones from a small gland at the base of the brain. The word 'puberty' comes from a Latin word, meaning to become covered in hair. But hair growth is only one of the changes that will happen to you as you go through puberty. You will also get taller, your body shape will change, girls' periods will begin and boys will start producing sperm. The way you think and act will change as well.

People go through puberty so that when they get older they can have children if they want to. For those of you who are thinking — 'I don't want children anyway' — going through puberty is nature's way of giving everyone the choice and ensuring that the human race continues. Puberty is part of growing up; everyone goes through it. Your parents have, so have your grandparents, teachers — even the Prime Minister! You won't reach puberty at exactly the same time as your friends do, and puberty will take different lengths of time for different people. However, it is helpful to realise that all people experience puberty.

The changes that happen to you at puberty usually happen very gradually. You may not be aware of these changes for a while, and then one day you'll notice that you're different. You look different and feel differently about all sorts of things. You may notice that your friends are changing too. Sometimes you realise that other people, such as your parents and family, start treating you differently, because you are growing up.

The reason we have written this book is because it is important for you to learn about all of these changes before they happen. It is also helpful if you have some idea how these changes may affect your life. The questions that we have used in this book are actual questions asked by the young people we have worked with. We have found that children from all different types of backgrounds ask the same sorts of questions, because what they are all going through is fairly similar.

Regardless of which country you or your parents come from, where you live or what religion you are, you will experience the same sorts of changes other people do. This doesn't mean that all people are alike. In fact, this is one of the most important points to learn and understand about puberty. We are all unique individuals who will experience things in our own way.

Knowledge can be very reassuring. It tells you that what you are experiencing is normal and OK. For example, some young people might feel confused about periods or wet dreams if they don't know what they are. They could think they have a disease! It's great if this reassurance can come from those who care about you and who are understanding — like your parents. Discussing how you are feeling and what you are experiencing with others will clarify these things in your own mind and help you realise that other people have had similar experiences. We hope this book will act as a trigger to help you talk with others about what is happening to you.

If you know and understand what is going on with your body and feelings, it usually makes any change a lot easier. That doesn't mean that you won't sometimes feel confused and unsure of yourself, but we hope the information in this book will help you keep things in perspective most of the time.

Kelsey Powell
Wendy Darvill

To the next generation
Archie, Greta and Rumi

Chapter 1

What's happening to my body?

How you feel about the changes that happen at puberty will depend on a number of things. If you have been well prepared with lots of information, you will know what to expect and be able to understand the changes as they happen.

Young people today are lucky when it comes to learning about puberty. Most schools teach students about puberty in their sexuality education programs, some from early primary school. Many parents are happy to talk to their children about puberty and growing up, and there is more information available on television, in books and on the internet.

It wasn't so long ago that most girls and boys were told nothing or very little about growing up. For many of your parents' generation the first thing they knew about puberty was when the changes actually happened.

1

Imagine knowing nothing about periods and going to the toilet and seeing blood on your underpants. Many women say how scared they were, thinking they were sick or bleeding to death! Similarly, imagine how confused a boy would be the first time he had a wet dream if he had never heard of them before. Occasionally, we still hear stories such as these, but fortunately it is becoming far less common.

> Sometimes the information young people receive about growing up can be fairly negative or misleading.

Sometimes the information young people receive about growing up can be fairly negative or misleading, and this may also influence how they feel. For example, periods aren't a big deal for most women. They manage them well and it doesn't stop them leading busy lives and doing all the things they want to do. However, if a girl hears from someone that periods are painful or a nuisance, this is what she will remember and perhaps tell her friends. Many boys are under the impression that a wet dream is like wetting the bed, because this is what they have heard. This is, of course, incorrect.

Try not to let other people's experiences scare you, as they may be exaggerated to make people feel sorry for them or to get attention. The physical changes you go through happen to everyone, but everyone experiences them a little differently, so wait and judge for yourself.

The physical changes that happen to girls

- Breasts develop
- Nipples stand out
- Hips (pelvis) become wider
- Hair grows under the arms, around the pubic area and increases slightly on arms and legs
- Body shape becomes more curvy as fat is deposited
- Genitals become darker in colour and fleshier
- Vaginal discharge becomes more noticeable
- Ovulation begins
- Periods start

The physical changes that happen to boys

- Shoulders and chest get broader
- Body becomes more muscular
- Breasts may temporarily grow a little
- Voice gets noticeably deeper
- Penis and testicles become larger and darker in colour. Sperm is produced
- Hair grows under the arms, around the pubic area, on arms and legs, face, chest and back
- During wet dreams or when masturbating, ejaculation may occur

The physical changes that happen to girls and boys

- Height suddenly increases
- Weight increases
- Face changes shape and fills out
- Skin becomes oilier
- Sweating increases
- Pimples may develop

Questions that relate to girls

(but would interest boys as well)

Is it normal to have dark pubic hair before developing breasts? — *girl, 13 years*

Pubic hair and breast development is different for everyone, so it's difficult to say what exactly is 'normal'. It is common for breasts to develop and pubic hair to grow at about the same time. Usually, breasts develop just a little earlier, but occasionally pubic hair may grow first. For some girls, early breast development may not be very noticeable.

> For some girls early breast development may not be very noticeable.

Did you know?

About breasts

- The main function of the breasts is to feed a baby. They are also important because they give a woman pleasure when touched, and many people find breasts sexually attractive.
- Breasts are mainly made up of fatty tissue and contain the mammary glands (which produce the milk).
- Oestrogen is the hormone that triggers breast development. It causes fat to be deposited and the ducts to grow. The ducts are where the milk will be stored if the woman has a baby.
- The average age for breast development is about 11, but starting a few years earlier or later is common.
- The area around the nipple, called the areola, is often the first part to change and will become darker and thicker. Then the nipple will grow and this whole area fills out a little. This is called the breast bud stage.
- Sometimes breasts may be tender, even a little painful, as they grow.
- One breast may develop before the other; however, they both end up being about the same size.

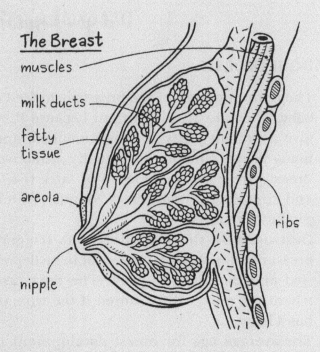

The Breast

muscles

milk ducts

fatty
tissue

areola

nipple

ribs

- Boys may experience some breast develop-ment as they go through puberty. This is quite common and soon disappears.
- The size of a female's breasts is determined mainly by heredity. That means the size of her breasts will probably be similar to her mother's or to the women in her father's family. There is nothing that can be done to make breasts grow larger. Females who do a lot of exercise may have firmer breasts or slightly smaller breasts because they have less body fat. The size of a woman's breasts will not affect her ability to breastfeed.

Why does it hurt when your breasts are developing? — *girl, 12 years*

Many girls experience breast tenderness and sometimes pain in the breasts. It is caused mainly by changing hormone levels and general growth of the breasts. Sometimes wearing a bra helps, particularly if your breasts are fairly large. Being hit in the breasts can be very painful. While this hurts at the time, it doesn't do any permanent damage.

What age are you when you start wearing a bra? — *girl, 9 years*

This will vary. You don't have to wear a bra unless you want to. If your breasts are well developed it may be more comfortable to wear one, especially when you are playing sport, dancing or running around a lot. As a woman ages it is natural for the elastic fibres in the breasts to stretch and for the breasts to sag a little. Wearing a bra won't stop this happening. If and when you decide to wear a bra, it is important to buy one that fits well; otherwise it may be uncomfortable. Shop around and try on a few. Just because a bra is expensive doesn't mean it is necessarily better.

What is the yellow stuff on my knickers? — *girl, 9 years*

If a girl touches around the outside or inside of her vagina she will find that it is moist. This is a lubricating fluid called mucus. It also helps to keep the vagina clean. The white or yellowish mark on your pants is this mucus, and perhaps fluid coming from the uterus. It is absolutely normal.

As you reach puberty the amount of vaginal mucus usually increases. It may become quite noticeable just before your first period starts, or at around the middle of your cycle (just before ovulation) if you already have your periods. It is usually clear, white or pale yellow. If the colour or amount changes a lot, or if your vulva becomes itchy or very smelly, you should see a doctor, because it could mean that you have an infection. Vaginal infections, particularly one called thrush, are quite common and are very easily treated.

Periods (menstruation)

At what age do you have periods?
— girl, 11 years

It is usual to start having periods somewhere between the ages of nine and 16. Between 11 and 13 years is average, but everyone is different. Periods nearly always start a year or two after other physical changes such as breast development or growth of pubic hair. The age at which a girl has her first period is often the age at which her mother had her first period. For the first year or two, your periods may be a little irregular, but they usually settle down and come about every 28 days. This will vary from female to female but the majority of cycles are between 25 and 31 days.

Did you know?

About the menstrual cycle

The word menstruation comes from the Latin word 'mensis', meaning month, because on average the period comes about once a month. That monthly 'period' is a cycle of events controlled by hormones.

Why do periods happen? — *girl, 10 years*

It's all to do with babies! Periods happen as a result of the hormones being released from a small gland at the base of the brain called the pituitary gland. These hormones cause an ovum (egg) to mature and to be released from the ovary. This is called ovulation. At the same time the lining of the uterus is thickening, so that if the ovum is fertilised it can embed itself in the lining and grow. It's a little like a soft bed waiting for a pregnancy to happen. Fertilisation can only happen if sperm joins with an ovum. If the ovum isn't fertilised the lining of the uterus will break down and the blood and tissue from the lining will come out through the vagina over the next five days or so — this is the period.

Once you get your periods it means that you may be physically able to become pregnant and have a baby. However, this doesn't mean you are mature enough to take on the responsibility of looking after a baby.

Menstruation

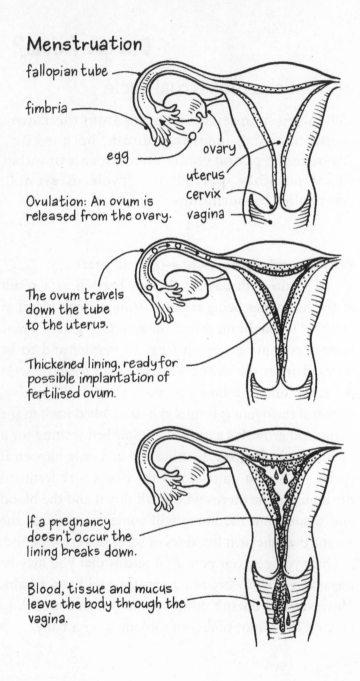

fallopian tube

fimbria

egg

ovary

uterus

cervix

vagina

Ovulation: An ovum is
released from the ovary.

The ovum travels
down the tube
to the uterus.

Thickened lining, ready for
possible implantation of
fertilised ovum.

If a pregnancy
doesn't occur the
lining breaks down.

Blood, tissue and mucus
leave the body through the
vagina.

Did you know?

About menstruation

- Menstrual flow is made up of tissue or cells from the lining of the uterus (called the endometrium), blood and mucus.
- The total loss for each period is about 100 ml or half a cup. Of this, approximately 35–60 ml, or about three tablespoons, is blood.
- Cycles may be irregular for the first year or two. Being worried, under stress, sick, or even going on holidays can cause periods to be late.
- The age of the first period in some countries has dropped by about four years in the last 100 years. This is probably due to the increased amount of protein in the diet, and better health care. However, the age is levelling out, so in another hundred years the average age will probably be about the same as it is now.
- A girl's period might stop or be delayed if she goes on a strict diet to maintain a very low body weight, or if she has anorexia nervosa. Women who play very strenuous sports and train for long periods, such as some ballet dancers or gymnasts, may also start their periods at a later age.
- A girl usually starts having periods between the ages of 11 and 13, although it could be earlier or later. Periods will then continue until she is about 50. This stage in a woman's life is called the menopause.

What does it feel like to have a period?
— *girl, 9 years*

Many girls feel virtually nothing except a slight trickling sensation every now and then. This might feel like a small bubble coming out of your vagina. Sometimes when a period begins you may feel some backache, or cramping in the pelvic area. It is usually mild and won't stop you doing the things you enjoy. If it is very painful you can take something like paracetamol or other medications available from the chemist, apply heat (a heat pack is good) or relax for a few hours. Some girls find gentle exercise gives relief. If these steps don't help it's probably worth seeing a doctor, just for a check-up.

How long does a period last for?
— *girl, 11 years*

The average length of a period is five days. The period can be as short as two days or up to seven days or longer. Each period is not always the same, so one month it may last for five days and the next month, six days.

Does it hurt when you insert a tampon for the first time? — *girl, 12 years*

Some girls are a little nervous about using a tampon for the first time. If this is the case the muscles around the vaginal opening may become tight, and inserting the tampon may be difficult. It is important to relax. Try taking a few deep breaths or wriggling your toes. Make sure you have privacy. Choose a time when you're not in a hurry, likely to be interrupted or under pressure in other ways. For the first time don't try just before going swimming or going out because if it feels uncomfortable you may want to adjust it or take it out. It is a good idea to use mini

There's no hurry!

tampons until you get used to inserting them and to try on days when your menstrual flow is heaviest; this will give you some lubrication. Alternatively, just for the first couple of times you could spread a little saliva (spit) or personal lubricant (like KY jelly, available from chemists and supermarkets) around the entrance of your vagina beforehand. This should help it slip in a bit more easily. Remember the vagina slopes up and towards your back, not straight up towards your chin. If it doesn't feel comfortable the first time, try again later — there's no hurry!

I've heard that it hurts pulling out a tampon after you've been swimming, because it expands.
— *girl, 13 years*
If a girl wears a tampon swimming, a small amount of water can enter the vagina and be absorbed by the tampon. But a tampon can only expand so far, and as the vagina is very elastic it should not hurt when it is removed. Remember, it's important to relax.

Did you know?

About pads and tampons

Pads

Pads or sanitary napkins are rectangles of absorbent material, like cottonwool. They have a plastic lining at the base and a fine, absorbent material on top. The base has a sticky strip that holds the pad onto your underpants. Pads come in different thicknesses for light- and heavy-flow days. Some are shaped to fit the body. All types of pads need to be changed at least every four hours through the day, sometimes more often if periods are heavy.

When you change a pad, don't flush it down the toilet because it is likely to block the plumbing. Some public toilets have special disposal units for pads and tampons. If there isn't one, or when you are at home, wrap the pad in some toilet paper or a paper bag and put it into the garbage bin.

Tampons

Tampons are like pads, except that the absorbent material is pressed together so that it is small enough to be worn inside the vagina. Tampons are inserted either with a cardboard applicator or with your finger. A string is firmly attached to one end for easy removal. The muscles of the vagina hold the tampon in place until you remove it. It can't fall out or disappear up inside you.

Like pads, you will need to change a tampon every three or four hours, or more often if your flow is heavy. Like pads, it is best to dispose of tampons in a disposal unit or by wrapping in paper and putting in a bin. Only flush down the toilet if there is no other choice.

It is a good idea to wear pads overnight rather than a tampon. Wearing tampons for extended lengths of time is not recommended because of the risk of Toxic Shock Syndrome.

Toxic Shock Syndrome (TSS)

Toxic Shock Syndrome is a very rare condition that is caused by an infection. To minimise the risk of TSS, tampon manufacturers recommend:

- Change tampons regularly throughout the day
- Take care with personal hygiene and wash your hands before and after inserting a tampon
- Avoid wearing a tampon overnight
- Avoid handling tampons more than necessary. Open just before using.

Since these recommendations have been put on tampon packets, the incidence of Toxic Shock has fallen. Toxic Shock Syndrome is not always caused by tampon use.

Pads or tampons — *your choice*

Some girls are happy to use pads all the time. Tampons, for some girls, do have advantages.

- They can be worn while swimming.
- Sometimes, particularly on very hot days, the menstrual flow on the pad dries and may develop a slight smell. As tampons are worn inside the body, this does not happen.
- No one can tell you are wearing a tampon, whereas the outline of a pad might be noticeable, especially under tight clothes such as leggings or bike pants.
- If a tampon is inserted correctly it cannot be felt. Some pads may feel a little bulky to wear.
- Tampons, because of their size, are more discreet. They can easily be carried in a pocket or purse.
- For some girls pads are easier to use because they are worn on the outside of the body.
- Pads or panty liners (small, thin pads) can be worn with tampons to give extra protection if a girl's menstrual flow is very heavy.

- Wearing pads at least some of the time allows you to become familiar with the amount of menstrual flow you experience. This will help you know how frequently to change your pad or tampon.
- Panty liners may be useful for extra security on the days before your period is due. The panty liner protects your underwear or clothing.
- All packets of pads and tampons include instructions for use. Read these carefully.

Most girls seem to start off using pads, and when they feel ready they try tampons. There is no hurry, and the choice is entirely up to you, although you might like to discuss it with your mum or another understanding adult.

What happens if a string of a tampon breaks?
— *girl, 10 years*

If you held a tampon and pulled on the string with all your strength you would find that it is extremely difficult to break. However, if this does happen, the tampon can be removed by inserting a finger and thumb into the vagina and pulling it out. This should not be difficult to do. Again, being relaxed will make it a lot easier.

Will I still be a virgin if I use tampons?
— *girl, 11 years*

Using tampons won't affect your virginity. It is generally agreed that a virgin is someone who has never had sexual intercourse. Some people link the loss of a girl's virginity with the breaking of her hymen, a thin piece of skin that may partly cover the entrance to the vagina. In nearly all girls there is already a gap to allow menstrual blood to flow out. This may be stretched wider when a girl uses tampons, or when she masturbates. Using a tampon doesn't usually break the hymen, although it may stretch it a little.

Can a nine-year-old have periods? Should she have some pads just in case? — *girl, 9 years*

Yes, girls as young as nine can get their periods. Usually they would have experienced other changes such as breast development and growth of pubic or underarm hair. If these changes are happening to you, it is a good idea to keep a pad or two handy, and perhaps a spare pair of underwear at school. You might like to keep them in a separate pencil case, a toiletry bag or lunch box, so that it won't be obvious if someone looks in your bag or when you need to take it to the toilet. If you are caught unaware, most schools keep a supply of pads at the school office or first aid room, or one of your friends may have one. If nothing else is available, you can use a hanky, some tissues or even some toilet paper until you can get a pad or tampon.

If a girl's wearing a pad, can it fall out of her undies or shorts? — *girl, 10 years*

No, it can't fall out. The pad is kept in place by a very sticky strip pressed onto your underwear. Try pressing the pad firmly onto your hand and then shake it about. You will find that it is very difficult for it to fall off. The elastic around the legs of your pants will also help to keep it in place.

What would you do if you had your period in class time? — *girl, 11 years*

The simplest thing would be to excuse yourself and get a pad or tampon from your bag on the way to the toilet. If you don't have a pad in your bag you could quietly ask one of your friends if she has one, and take it from her bag. Otherwise you will need to go to the office or first aid room. Most teachers are very sensitive to the needs and the privacy of young girls at puberty.

Remember that teachers have all gone through puberty themselves. A female teacher would know about periods from personal experience, and most male teachers would be understanding. Many would have a wife, girlfriend, sister or mother and would know something about menstruation.

Can you start or get your period in your sleep?
— girl, 11 years
Periods can start at any time of the day or night. Sometimes if they start during the night you will wake up soon after they start, but you may not wake until morning. Your sheets and pyjamas may have some blood on them, but this will wash out quite easily in *cold* water.

Is it true that girls can't go swimming for a couple of days when they've got their periods?
— girl, 12 years
There is no physical reason why you can't go swimming or play sport while you have your period. However, you can't wear a pad when swimming and wearing no protection will mean that your swimsuit would get blood on it. You would need to wear a tampon if you want to go swimming when you have your period.

What is PMS? *— girl, 13 years*
PMS stands for pre-menstrual syndrome. It is a group of symptoms that can occur for the week or so before

Did you know?

Tips if you get blood on your clothes

- Sponge it off with cold water on a cloth, tissue or toilet paper.
- If a jumper is available perhaps you could tie that around your waist until you can change your clothes.
- Carry a spare pair of pants in your school bag.
- Many schools have a number of spare uniforms for 'accidents' — ask at the office or a teacher you feel comfortable with.

a period and during the first days of the period. PMS is probably caused by an imbalance of hormones. Many females notice some minor changes just before their period is due, and for a small percentage of females the symptoms are quite severe. The type of symptoms you might experience include a bloated or painful abdomen, tender or sore breasts, headache, backache and pimples. You might feel tired or irritable. There are other less common symptoms, and all symptoms will vary from female to female and sometimes from month to month.

For most girls PMS is not a major problem and doesn't stop them doing the things they normally enjoy.

What can help prevent or relieve PMS?
— *girl, 13 years*
If you experience symptoms of PMS that distress you, it would be a good idea to see your doctor just to make sure that everything is OK. If PMS is the problem, there are a number of things you can do. Having a healthy diet is a good start. Gentle exercise, such as swimming or walking, also helps many women. Relaxation is important, and avoiding situations that are likely to upset you may help. You may also find taking Vitamin B6 can help. Sometimes painkillers are necessary for those who experience pain and discomfort.

Do you get frustrated with your mum just before you start your period? — *girl, 13 years*
When you are in a bad mood, for whatever reason, you tend to take it out on the people you see or love most. This might be Mum, Dad, a brother or sister or friend — maybe even your dog! Rather than getting angry and shouting, try talking about how you are feeling. This often helps you to feel better, and it also helps others to understand.

Questions that relate to boys

(but will interest girls as well)

How are sperm made? — *boy, 11 years*
Sperm are made in response to a hormone released by the pituitary gland. This triggers the production

of testosterone in the testicles, which is necessary for the sperm to mature. The sperm are made inside the testicles and mature in tubes called the epididymis, which lie over each testicle. The sperm then move through the vas and mix with fluids that come from other glands. These fluids include proteins, enzymes and lubricants that nourish the sperm and help them move more easily. This fluid, mixed with the sperm, is called semen.

What's a wet dream? — boy, 10 years
A wet dream is when you have an erection and ejaculate while you are asleep. It might be because you have had a sexy dream or maybe you weren't dreaming at all. Wet dreams happen once your body starts producing sperm. Only a certain amount can be stored, so a wet dream is a way for some to escape. The amount of fluid is only about 5 ml or one teaspoonful, so it isn't as if you've wet the bed. You can clean up with tissues, a wet face washer or just put your undies or pyjamas in the wash. It's unlikely that there will be so much mess that the sheets need washing, but if they do, it's nothing to be embarrassed about. Remember, this happens to all boys as they mature.

How old are you when you have wet dreams? — boy, 11 years
It's difficult to say exactly, because it's different for everybody. On average it's about 13, but it could be younger or older.

Did you know?

About semen and ejaculation

- Sperm start to be produced in the testicles about a year after the penis and testicles start to grow.
- Ejaculation is when the semen, the fluid that contains the sperm, comes out of the erect penis. It may happen when a boy masturbates or has a wet dream, or during sexual intercourse.
- The amount of semen in each ejaculation is about 5 ml or one teaspoonful and in a mature man contains between 200 and 500 million sperm.
- It would take 1 million sperm to fit on the head of a pin.
- A mature sperm is approximately .05 mm long. It is similar in shape to a tadpole and has an oval head that allows it to penetrate the ovum (egg). The tail of the sperm moves from side to side, allowing it to move up through the uterus towards the fallopian tube, which might contain an ovum.
- A young man usually ejaculates for the first time between the ages of 12 and 14, although he may be younger or older.

What is the level of wet dreaming?
— *boy, 12 years*

Again, that's different for every boy. It may only ever happen a couple of times, or it might happen a few times a week. If you masturbate and ejaculate often, you may not have as many wet dreams as a boy who doesn't masturbate.

What does a wet dream feel like?
— *boy, 12 years*

When you have a wet dream and ejaculate you will usually have an orgasm, and this will give a very pleasurable sensation. This is when the muscles in the penis contract to push the fluid out of the penis. You may wake up almost straight away, or you may not realise you have ejaculated until you notice a bit of a white mark on your pants or on the sheets in the morning.

When boys have a wet dream does it smell?
— boy, 12 years

Sperm has a very slight odour, which would be hardly noticeable after a wet dream. It is certainly not an unpleasant smell, so it's not something to be worried about.

Do girls have wet dreams? *— boy, 13 years*

Girls don't have wet dreams in the same way that boys do, because they don't produce sperm. However, some will have dreams in which they have strong sexual feelings and sensations, which they may remember in the morning. During these dreams a girl's vagina may become quite moist.

Why do boys' voices break? *— boy, 10 years*

Just as the rest of your body grows, so too does your larynx (voice box). You have probably noticed that men have a lump or Adam's apple in the middle of their throat. This is the larynx, and as it grows the voice becomes deeper. Usually this happens fairly gradually and the change isn't obvious, but for some boys it's quite quick. Now and then your voice might sound a little strange; this is called cracking or breaking. It could be a little embarrassing, particularly if you are talking to someone you are trying to impress. If it's happening a lot try speaking in a low, even voice, without too many high notes. This might help.

Girls' voices change as well, but not as much or as noticeably.

When do I get my muscles? — *boy, 12 years*

Muscles develop gradually over a number of years as you go through puberty. How muscular you will be depends on a number of things: the amount and type of sport you play, whether you have a healthy diet and the type of body shape you have. If you have a very slight frame, although exercise will add more to your muscles it's unlikely that you will ever look like Arnold Schwarzenegger. Everyone is different and your body shape will be great because it belongs to you!

Why does a boy's penis go stiff?
— *boy, 11 years*

A penis gets stiff because more blood flows into it than flows out and this causes it to become stiff and stand away from the body. An erect penis is quite a bit bigger than a soft (flaccid) one. The correct name is an erection; some slang names are 'a hard on' or a 'boner'. An erection is necessary for a man to have sexual intercourse. When a male's penis becomes erect, muscles at the base of the bladder (where the urine is stored) tighten up so that he can't urinate while he's having sex. It's a little like turning off the tap for a while!

I get erections all the time — for no reason. Why?
— *boy, 13 years*

All males get erections. Even little baby boys get them now and then if they are about to urinate, or if they or someone else touches their penis or testicles. As you grow up, erections will become more common. Touching your penis may cause it to become erect, and so might movement or vibration like being on a bus or train. Thinking sexy thoughts, watching movies with love scenes or looking at pictures of naked or sensual bodies may also lead to an erection. Sometimes erections happen for no reason at all. This is called a spontaneous erection and for some young men it can happen quite often.

> If this happens to you, the best thing you can do is to concentrate on something really boring.

If this happens to you, the best thing you can do is to concentrate on something really boring, like what you had for breakfast, or doing some maths in your head, to make the erection go away. If you're finding your erections embarrassing you could try to disguise them by wearing loose clothing like tracksuit pants, or tight jeans to hold the penis down. When you go swimming, wear board shorts rather than tight trunks.

What do you do if your penis is small?
— *boy, 13 years*
Penis size varies from male to male, and because all boys mature at different rates, some boys of 13 might have a small penis, while a few may have a large penis. All penises will grow given time.

Some boys can be very cruel and tease other boys about the size of their penis. This is quite ridiculous, because having a bigger penis doesn't mean a boy is more of a man. In fact, a penis will do exactly the same job whatever size it is. The size of a man's penis has little to do with the quality of sex — for either men or women.

Once a penis is erect the size evens out to some extent. This means that a fairly small penis will enlarge more than a big penis.

When can you start to shave or grow a beard?
— *boy, 13 years*
You can start to shave as soon as hairs appear on your face, if you want to. This usually happens between the ages of 14 and 18. Some early developers may need to shave every day by the time they are 16, while some men may never grow a really thick beard. Often hair appears first above your top lip and on the chin. It's light and fluffy to start with and gets darker and coarser as you get older. The colour of your facial hair (beard or moustache) may be different from your pubic hair or the hair on your head. Many young men see shaving as a sign of being grown up, and look forward to their first shave. Some men may choose not to shave.

My dad is really hairy. Does that mean I will be too?
— *boy, 10 years*
Some men are very hairy, with pubic hair that goes up to their navel, hairy chests and faces, even hairy backs. In fact, some men seem to have hair everywhere except on the tops of their heads! Other men may not

be very hairy, and some adult men don't even need to shave each day. The amount of body hair we have is a characteristic we usually inherit from our parents. There is a good chance that if your dad is hairy you will be too, unless you take after a grandfather or uncle who isn't so hairy. Some men may choose to shave their body hair.

I still haven't got any pubic hair. Is this OK?
— boy, 14 years
This is quite normal. Everyone develops at different rates. The rate that you develop is right for you.

Can boys get breasts as well? — girl, 12 years
Some boys experience minor breast development when they start going through puberty. Their hormones settle down within a year or so, and the breast development goes away. If this is happening to you and you are worried about being teased, avoid wearing tight-fitting T-shirts or shirts.

Questions that relate to boys and girls

At what age are you fully developed?
— girl, 12 years
On average, girls have finished growing when they are about 17 and boys have reached their adult height

by about 19. Different parts of the body, such as the breasts and the penis, would probably have reached their maximum size a few years before this. Complete reproductive maturity is reached two or three years after final adult height is reached.

Can you explain what a hormone is?
— *boy, 11 years*
A hormone is a chemical produced in the body. It is released into the blood to control the body and its functions. As you go through puberty, hormones are responsible for the changes you experience. During puberty the main hormones are oestrogen and progesterone in girls and testosterone in boys. The production of these hormones is controlled by a gland in the brain called the pituitary.

Is it all right if some pubic hairs are much longer than others? — *boy, 12 years*
Yes, some pubic hairs can be longer than others, particularly when they first start to grow. Some will be quite short and fine for a while, but eventually they thicken up and the length will even out a little, although they won't all be the same.

How come I get pimples? — *girl, 11 years*
From puberty a fatty substance called sebum is released from the pores of the skin. For a time there may be too much sebum and the pores may block up. This causes pimples or blackheads.

Did you know?

About pubic hair

- Pubic hair is hair that grows around the genitals. Fully grown, it forms a triangle shape but for many men and some women it extends in a line up to the navel.
- It starts growing soft and fine and light in colour, then becomes more coarse and dark as you get older.
- Pubic hair may be a different colour from the hair on your head — it is usually darker.
- The amount of pubic hair varies from person to person, as does all body hair. Some people are very hairy and others are not. Some cultural groups, such as Southern Europeans, may have quite a lot of dark body hair, while many Asian people are not very hairy at all. Neither is better or worse — it is just the way we are.

What's the best way to get rid of pimples?
— boy, 14 years

Keeping your skin clean is the best way to stop or clear up pimples. This doesn't mean using lots of expensive cleansers. Washing twice a day with a mild, unperfumed soap and warm water, or a mild anti-bacterial wash from the chemist, should be enough. It's not a good idea to scrub your face too hard — this can cause more pimples by stimulating oil production. Creams that help dry out existing pimples might be helpful,

and they can also be purchased from the chemist and most large supermarkets. Having a healthy diet, exercising and drinking plenty of water may also help, as do sunlight (but not sunburn) and fresh air.

Squeezing pimples can actually spread infection and damage the skin. If you have to, only squeeze blackheads, and make sure both your hands and face are very clean. If your pimples are very bad it may be a good idea to see a doctor. Occasionally, antibiotics or other medications may be helpful.

Have people found reasons for people maturing faster than others? — boy, 12 years

The main reason is heredity, that is, the characteristics we inherit from our parents. Diet also plays a part and people who are very poorly nourished may not develop as early as people who have plenty to eat. If a girl is involved in very strenuous exercise for long periods of time (like gymnasts or ballet dancers) then the onset of puberty may be delayed. Exercise does not influence the onset of puberty in boys in the same way. Puberty may also be delayed for people who suffer from anorexia nervosa.

Why do you get clumsy when you're going through puberty? — *boy, 11 years*

The parts of your body won't all grow at the same rate. For a while your arms and legs may be out of proportion to the rest of your body. Your feet, hands and sometimes your nose might also appear overly large for a while. Eventually all of your body parts will even out, but until then you might feel a little awkward and be a bit clumsy at times. You may trip over now and then and drop things. Your height may change rapidly as well, which might take a little getting used to. If you do become clumsy, try slowing down a little to give yourself the chance to think about your movements.

Do all people go through puberty? — *girl, 11 years*

Yes, everyone will go through puberty as they grow from being a girl to a woman or a boy to a man. Puberty is a natural process that enables us to have children.

For you to think about

Feelings about your changing body

Many people worry about what others think of them, and are always comparing themselves to others. For young people this may be a real issue as they don't want to stand out or be different for fear of being teased or laughed at. There is often a lot of pressure to look and dress a certain way. This pressure can come from a whole lot of places, including TV, movies, radio, the fashion industry, your friends and your parents. It is important to remember that everyone is different; everyone is an individual.

Boys and girls who go through puberty earlier or later than others may feel different from their peer group. Early developers aren't any better than late developers, and being a later developer doesn't mean you are less intelligent or will be less of a man or woman. By the time you are in your late teens things will have evened out.

If people are teasing you, think about the reasons behind their behaviour. Are they jealous of you? Are they trying to impress you or someone else? For some people, teasing is the only way they know to get another person's attention. Perhaps they are showing how insecure *they* are about what is happening to *them*. ☞

Be proud of your body. It can already do so much — think, play sport, dance, hug the people you love, write and create. You will still be able to do all those things, but more and even better.

Puberty is a time of growing up and a time to be proud of. It means that you are maturing and growing into a man or a woman, and this is pretty special. It also means that one day, if you want to, you can have children and become a mum or a dad yourself and this is wonderful — just ask your parents!

For you to discuss with a parent or an adult who cares about you

What their experiences of puberty were. How they managed pimples, periods, wet dreams or buying their first bra.

Where they learnt about puberty. Was it from their parents, from friends or from older brothers or sisters?

Share with them how you feel about your changing body. Talking with someone who cares can really help.

Chapter 2

Understanding male and female bodies

Although the way you change at puberty will affect you physically, socially and emotionally, the most obvious changes are the physical ones. These have been discussed in detail in the previous chapter. To better understand these changes we need to know something about male and female bodies, especially the reproductive systems.

If you know and understand what your body looks like and how it works, you are more likely to feel more comfortable with it and therefore with yourself in general. Also, knowing about your body will help you look after it and keep it healthy. This is especially so when you are older and perhaps in a sexual relationship, or if ever you choose to have a baby.

It is also good to learn about people of the other sex so you can know what is happening to them. This will help you to understand what they are experiencing and how they may be feeling.

The female body

The female reproductive system includes the breasts and the genital area. Most of the female reproductive organs are inside the body, whereas the male's are on the outside. For this reason it is more difficult for females to actually see all their genital area. Girls might need to use a mirror to get a good look at their genitals.

The external sex organs

The genital area on the outside is called the vulva. At the top of the vulva is a mound of fatty tissue (which

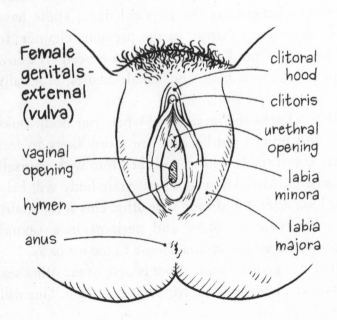

Female genitals - external (vulva)

clitoral hood
clitoris
urethral opening
vaginal opening
labia minora
hymen
anus
labia majora

Did you know?

About fish

Some types of fish actually change sex — they may be male for some years and then change to female or vice versa.

becomes covered with hair at puberty) called the mons pubis. Below this are two folds of skin called the labia majora (or outer lips) and labia minora (or inner lips). The labia majora are also covered with hair after puberty. When the girl's legs are together the labia majora lie close together; the labia minora can only be seen if her legs are apart. The labia minora are thinner than the labia majora and are sensitive to touch. They are also moist, because a lubricating fluid is produced by glands in the labia.

At the top of the labia minora is the clitoris. The clitoris has many nerve endings and is the most sensitive part of the female genital area. Only the tip of the clitoris is visible on the outside and its size will vary from female to female. The labia minora form a fold of skin or hood over the clitoris. When a girl or woman is sexually aroused, the clitoris becomes more exposed and firm.

Inside the labia minora are two openings. The opening at the front is the urethral opening (the urethra is a small tube that carries the urine from the bladder to the outside). The other opening is the vaginal opening, which is larger than the urethral opening and leads to the vagina.

The internal organs
The vagina The vagina is a muscular tube about 10 centimetres long, leading to the uterus (or womb). Menstrual blood passes through the vagina. The sides of the vagina touch each other, and are creased. These muscles hold a tampon in place if a girl uses them

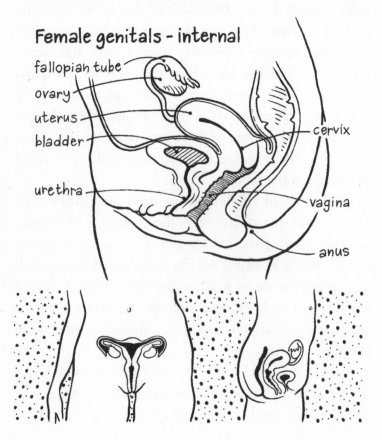

Female genitals - internal

fallopian tube
ovary
uterus
bladder
urethra
cervix
vagina
anus

Did you know?

About the hymen

In some cultures it was common for a couple's bed to be inspected the morning after their marriage. This was to find the evidence of blood from the torn hymen on the sheets. This was supposed to prove that the bride was a virgin and had not had sex before she married.

during her period. During childbirth the vagina can stretch a great deal to allow the baby through. Glands in the vagina produce a fluid that helps keep the vagina clean and moist. When a female is sexually aroused the vagina becomes wider, longer and more moist.

When a girl is born the entrance of her vagina is sometimes partially covered by a very thin piece of skin called the hymen. During puberty the vagina grows, and the hymen may stretch and tear. It may also stretch or tear when a girl plays sport, masturbates or uses tampons. Even if the hymen is not torn before puberty, small holes in it allow the menstrual blood to come out. When the woman has sexual intercourse for the first time the hymen may tear and even bleed a little. If this happens the woman may experience slight pain or tenderness the first time she has sex. The pain or discomfort should be only mild if she is sexually aroused and she and her partner take sex slowly.

The uterus The uterus (or womb) is a hollow organ low down in the female's abdomen. It sits behind the bladder. The uterus has thick muscular walls that sit close together and is where a baby grows and develops. The uterus is about the size and shape of a small upside-down pear and stretches a great deal to accommodate a growing baby. The bottom part of the uterus is connected to the vagina and is called the cervix.

> From the time a girl reaches puberty one ovum matures and is released each month.

The fallopian tubes Two fallopian tubes join the top of the uterus, one on each side. The fallopian tubes are about 10 centimetres long. Where they join the uterus they are narrow, about the width of spaghetti. They widen into a funnel shape which has finger-like endings. These endings, called fimbria, wrap around the ovary without actually touching it. When an ovum (egg) is released from the ovary the fimbria guide it into the fallopian tube.

The ovaries The ovaries, one on either side of the uterus, are two small oval-shaped organs that contain ova (eggs). The ovaries are about 2.5 centimetres long. When a girl is born there are thousands of ova in her ovaries.

Did you know?

About fertility

Most female animals continue to produce young throughout their lives, although they may be less fertile. Some large species of fish produce about five million ova at each spawning.

From the time a girl reaches puberty one of these ova matures and is released each month. The ovaries also produce important hormones called oestrogen and progesterone. These are the sex hormones that cause the changes that take place at puberty.

The ovaries continue to release ova and produce hormones until a woman reaches menopause, usually around the age of fifty. After this time a woman can no longer have a baby — although recently a number of women of this age have had babies with the help of medical intervention.

The breasts Female hormones released at puberty cause breast development. The main function of the breasts is to produce milk for feeding babies. Breasts are very sensitive to touch and many women get a lot of sexual pleasure from stimulation of the breasts.

The male body

It's easier for a boy to see his reproductive organs, as they are mainly on the outside.

The penis The penis has three functions: passing urine, passing semen (containing sperm) and giving sexual pleasure. The tip or head of the penis is called the glans and is the most sensitive part. The long part of the penis is called the shaft. The penis is made of

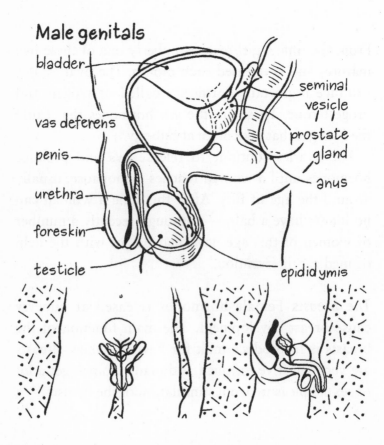

Male genitals

bladder

vas deferens

penis

urethra

foreskin

testicle

seminal vesicle

prostate gland

anus

epididymis

Did you know?

About penis size

The size of the penis when it is not erect varies from one man to another. It doesn't have anything to do with the man's body size. When a penis becomes erect, a small penis will increase in size more than a large penis. Therefore there is not as much difference in the size of erect penises.

nerve endings and a spongy material called erectile tissue. When a boy or man becomes sexually aroused the amount of blood going to the penis increases and small chambers inside the penis fill up with blood. This makes the penis hard and erect. The penis also becomes larger and darker in colour.

The foreskin is a fold of skin that covers the glans. Small glands under the foreskin produce a white, creamy substance called smegma. This allows the foreskin to slide easily over the glans of the penis. On the underside of the penis is a band of tissue called the fraenulum. This stops the foreskin being pulled too far back.

Some males have the foreskin removed, so that the glans of the penis will be exposed. This operation is called circumcision and is done for a variety of reasons.

For some people it has religious or cultural significance. A doctor or tribal elder may perform the operation soon after birth, or when the boy reaches puberty as a sign of manhood. Some parents have their sons circumcised because they believe it is cleaner, or because they think it is the right thing to do.

The testicles The testicles (or testes) are two glands that hang behind the penis in a bag of skin called the scrotum. One testicle hangs slightly lower than the

Did you know?

About the echidna's penis

Male echidna have their reproductive organs inside their body and the penis is a four-headed organ with each head able to release semen.

other so that they fit more comfortably. The testicles are divided into about 250 small segments, a bit like an orange. Each segment is made up of very tiny tubes, all curled up. Straightened out, they would measure many metres. The inside of these tubes is lined with cells and the sperm are produced in these when a boy has reached puberty. Once this process starts, about 70 million are produced continually each day right into old age.

Each sperm takes about 70 days to develop. The sperm move from the small tubes in the testicles and into the epididymis, which is a coiled tube that lies over the back of each testicle. The sperm are stored in the epididymis, where they continue to mature, for about 14 days.

The testicles also produce the sex hormone testosterone. This hormone causes the male characteristics, such as body hair, a deeper voice and more muscle. This hormone starts to be produced when a boy is about 12 and causes the changes that happen at puberty.

The sex hormone testosterone causes the changes that happen to a boy at puberty.

The scrotum The testicles are contained in a bag of skin called the scrotum. The scrotum plays an important part in sperm production by controlling the temperature of the testicles. Sperm can only be produced at a temperature that is a couple of degrees lower than the internal body temperature. The testicles hang on the outside of the body so that air circulates around them and keeps them slightly cooler than the rest of the body. When the outside temperature is cold the scrotum becomes smaller and brings the testicles closer to the body for more warmth. When the weather is hot or a man has just had a hot shower or has a fever,

the scrotum relaxes and
as a result the testicles
hang further away from
the body and become
cooler. The scrotum also
tightens up to protect
the testicles when a man
is frightened.

The scrotum plays an
important part in
sperm production by
controlling the temper-
ature of the testicles.

The vas The sperm move from the epididymis into tubes called the vas (or vas deferens), one connected to each testicle. These tubes transport the sperm into a storage area in the prostate gland. The prostate gland is about the size of a walnut and produces a fluid that helps the movement of sperm. There are other glands nearby — the seminal vesicles, which produce a substance that provides the sperm with nourishment, and the Cowper's glands, which produce lubricating fluid. This mixture of sperm and other fluid is called semen.

The two vas join together near the prostate gland and become a single tube called the urethra. The urethra has two functions. Firstly, it carries urine from the bladder to the outside of the body; secondly, it carries semen to the outside.

When a boy or man has an erection and ejaculates semen, a muscle closes off the urethra from the bladder to make sure urine does not mix with the semen. This is why it is difficult for a male to pass urine when he has an erection. Men sometimes have to wait until their erection goes away before they can pass urine.

Did you know?

About animal genitals

With some animals, such as the spotted hyena and the echidna, you cannot easily tell whether they are male or female because the male's and female's external genitals look the same.

Only the healthiest sperm make it to the urethra. Sperm that don't mature usually die in the epididymis. When a mature man ejaculates there are about 200 to 500 million sperm in approximately 5 ml of semen. Such large numbers are produced to make it more likely that fertilisation will take place if the semen is ejaculated into the vagina. The sperm also must be able to move very efficiently to make their way through the vagina and uterus and into the fallopian tubes.

Chapter 3

Learning to live with others

As well as all the physical changes you will experience at puberty, there are also emotional and social changes. The way you think about things and your relationships with others will change as well. This will include your relationship with your parents, brothers and sisters, friends and classmates. Many young people at puberty want to spend more time with their friends and less time with their parents and family. You might want to spend more time on your own just thinking or daydreaming.

This is a normal and necessary part of growing up, but it may be confusing at times, both for you and the people around you. Sometimes it is helpful to think about how you are getting on with the people you care about and how you might be able to improve the relationships you have with your family members and friends.

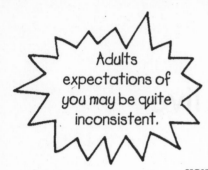

Adults expectations of you may be quite inconsistent.

As you get older you might find that adults' expectations of you may be quite inconsistent. For example, you may be expected to be responsible one minute, but then told you are too young to make your own decisions the next. These mixed messages may be quite confusing at times. Growing up is a gradual process and it takes adults and young people time to adjust. These conflicting messages will become fewer as you get older — it just takes time. If this is a problem for you, try discussing your concerns with the particular adult to help this person understand how you are feeling.

Parents

Because of the changing relationship between you and your parents, there can sometimes be a period of misunderstanding during puberty. You may want to have more independence, but your parents may worry that you are not mature enough or ready to cope with this independence and to make decisions for yourself. Some parents worry more than others and will be a lot more strict with their children, while other parents will be more relaxed and allow their children more freedom. Whichever way it is for you and your parents, they are just doing what they believe is best for you.

I think I would be embarrassed to tell my mum about these things. — *girl, 12 years*

Sometimes it is embarrassing to talk about growing up and changing feelings because it is personal. In some families these things are not talked about very often. If this is the case in your family, the best thing is to pick a time when you can sit down and talk privately to your mum or dad. They may be a little embarrassed, as their parents may not have talked to them about puberty, so you may need to give them a little time to get used to talking about these things. Most parents do want their children to come to them to discuss these things. Once you start it does become easier!

Remember, your parents have had quite a few years with you being very dependent on them and it may take them a while to get used to you becoming more independent.

Did you know?

Parents are changing too

As parents see their children growing up and becoming more independent, they often realise that they are getting older as well. This makes some parents stop and think about their lives, and they may wonder if they are doing what they want to and if they have achieved what they set out to achieve when they were younger. This might make them feel a little dissatisfied and they may think about wanting to make some changes in their lives. Young people need to be understanding about how their parents may be feeling.

Remember, parents are people too!

My parents are always picking on me. They don't like the way I dress and are always criticising me.
— *girl, 13 years*

Your parents' ideas of how they want you to look may differ from your ideas. You may want to experiment with how you look until you find a particular style you like, and this is a normal part of growing up. Often this may not be what your parents had in mind for you. This may result in you and your parents arguing about the way you dress. Maybe you could sit down with your parents and tell them how you feel, and that it is important to you to have the freedom to choose what you wear. It is best if you can discuss this calmly with your parents and not get angry.

Why won't my parents let me go out on a date?
— boy, 12 years

Many parents may feel that someone of this age is too young to go on a proper date and that it's better for you to wait until you are older. They probably think you are not ready to be involved with just one person. Maybe they would feel OK about you going out with a group of friends rather than one person, or they may rather you have friends around to your house. This way they will get to know your friends and maybe will eventually feel more comfortable with you going out with them. Why not sit down with your parents and discuss what their concerns are?

Talking to parents If you do want to ask your parents to let you do something new, like going to a movie or into town with a friend, find a suitable time to sit down and discuss it with them. It's not always a good idea to ask Dad or Mum when they are really busy or discussing something else. You may need to arrange a time with them. Think about your plans, like how are you going to get there and what time you think you'll be home. You may need to compromise. Perhaps one parent could drive you there, or pick you up at a certain time. Try and discuss it without getting angry. This will show your parents that you are mature enough and responsible enough to be allowed to do what you are asking.

Brothers and sisters

How come my brother and I are always fighting?
— *girl, 12 years*

Some brothers and sisters get on better than others. Just because people are related doesn't mean they are always going to be the best of friends. As you get older your relationship with your brother or sister may change. You may become closer to them, or you may find them frustrating and get on each other's nerves.

It's not fair to expect your parents to take sides and sort it out for you all the time. It's often a good idea to give each other a bit of time out if you are feeling annoyed. Get away from each other and cool down. You may even find that after a time you have both forgotten whatever you were upset about. If you haven't, try to talk about it without getting really cheesed off again.

I have a teenage sister. She hates me. Why is she always mean? — *girl, 10 years*

As your sister gets older she may want to be more independent, and this may mean not wanting to have as much to do with your family. This does not mean that she doesn't love you or the rest of your family. Also, when people reach puberty there is an increase in the hormones in their body. This may be making her feel a little moody at times. As you get older you may start to notice some of these changes in you.

Did you know?

About arguing with brothers and sisters

All brothers and sisters will argue at some time, some more than others. Arguing doesn't mean you don't like each other.

Arguing, to some extent, is a normal part of learning about getting on with others.

It can:

- teach you ways to express your feelings
- help you be more assertive (that's different from aggressive)
- give you the opportunity to express yourself in a safe environment
- teach you appropriate and inappropriate ways of behaving

Some people argue because they enjoy a heated discussion. Others may argue to get attention. For example your little brother or sister might constantly bother you when you are in the middle of doing your homework or listening to your favourite music. They do this because they want you to spend some time with them.

Your sister may just need some time on her own. You may like to tell her how you feel and talk about it with her. Pick a time when she is OK and not in a bad mood. When you are older you may have more in common and become closer.

Sometimes I get really angry and I lose my temper. I just can't help it. — *boy, 13 years*

Sudden changes in moods are quite common around puberty. Your anger could be caused by changes in hormone levels. If you're really angry and you feel that you're about to lose your temper, try counting to 10, or taking a few deep breaths.

There is nothing wrong with people disagreeing with each other. However, if they get very angry they may say things that they don't really mean, or make the other person angry as well, and that won't help the situation at all. Sometimes the only way to prevent a blow-up is to walk away.

When you're angry about something, try to stick to that particular issue. Say what is upsetting you and try to sort one problem out at a time. Avoid personal insults or bringing up past disagreements.

Friends

Friendships may also go through changes at this time. You may want to spend a lot of time with your friends and may feel closer to them in some ways than to your family. Friends will probably start to play a bigger

part in your life. This is an important part of growing up, as it will help you learn how to get on with others and how to be part of a group. The friendships you had when you were young might not have lasted a long time, but as you get older you usually become closer to your friends and your friendships may be more stable.

Some people think that to be friends you have to always think and feel the same way as each other. It is OK to disagree with your friends sometimes. In fact, it can be a lot healthier and more interesting if friends don't always agree, and if they feel comfortable discussing their different ideas on certain things.

For many young people at this time it might be important to belong to a particular group. They often want to identify as much as possible with their friends.

Did you know?

About groups

Sometimes groups have a set of rules about things like dress and language, and you might feel that to be accepted into a particular group you will have to stick by these rules. If you don't feel comfortable with these rules you don't have to follow them. Most people will respect you for being your own person. If they don't, you may want to think about whether you really want to be part of that group.

Doing things in a group may be more fun, and you may do things that you would not normally do if you were on your own. For example, you may have a cigarette because your friends are smoking. This is called peer pressure.

Sometimes peer pressure can be positive; it may mean you do something you've always wanted to do but never had the confidence to do, for example, going to the shops alone, going roller skating, going on a scary ride at a theme park, abseiling. Trying new things as you grow up helps you to feel good about yourself. However, it is important not to be talked into doing something that you don't want to do, or that may be wrong.

Parents and friends

Sometimes parents find it a little difficult to get used to their child's desire for more independence. They may feel hurt and confused about why their child doesn't want to spend as much time with them. Parents usually realise that this is the end of childhood, but also may feel their child is rejecting them and feel hurt.

You may be able to help your parents through this stage by letting them know that you still love them. Sometimes parents need reassurance too!

Parents may disapprove of some of your friends, and worry about the influence these friends have on you. Your parents will probably be reassured if you bring your friends home to give them the opportunity to meet and get to know them.

> People grow and mature at different times and in different ways.

My best friend really likes this boy and she talks about him all the time. I find it a bit boring sometimes. — *girl, 12 years*

People grow and mature at different times and in different ways, so you won't always have exactly the same interests as your friends. Some young people will become very interested in the other sex and thinking about them will take up a great deal of time. Maybe

For you to think about

Friendships

Here are some things that people think are important in a friendship. Which ones do you think are the most important?

- Being able to trust each other
- Having fun together
- Being honest with each other
- Being loyal to each other
- Being good looking
- Helping each other out
- Having lots in common
- Being smart
- Keeping each other company

Think about the things you like about your friends and the things that friends might like about you.

you could let your friend know how you feel, or maybe you can begin to spend time with some of your other friends.

Why do boys tease us about breasts?
— girl, 12 years

Often people tease when they don't understand about something, or when they feel embarrassed. Boys are usually a bit later reaching puberty than girls, and may

behave in a less mature way at times. They might feel a little anxious about the fact that they are not growing as quickly as they would like. Also some boys may be beginning to feel attracted to girls, and perhaps they are behaving in this way to get the girl's attention.

Sometimes you can stop people from teasing by letting them know how you feel. Tell the boys you do not like them teasing and you want them to stop doing it. If this doesn't work, just try to ignore them.

Why do people laugh when you put your arm around your friend or somebody accidentally touches you? — *girl, 11 years*
Often people laugh when they feel embarrassed or confused about what is happening. People at puberty often begin to feel differently about their relationships with others, but they may not feel comfortable

expressing these feelings. They may actually like the idea of touching or being touched, but feel a bit embarrassed about this. When they see other people being physically close, or if they accidentally touch someone, they may laugh to cover up their embarrassment or to hide their true feelings.

Making friends on social media

Social media is a great way to stay in touch with friends but there can be risks. Some people say and do things online that they would never consider doing face to face. They may post photos that are OK for friends to see but not really appropriate to be shared with people they don't know. Once something is put on the internet you don't have any control over who sees it.

It is important not to share personal information such as your account details or where you live. This information may be used inappropriately by people you don't know. Remember, it is easy for people to lie online, so you need to think carefully about how well you really know the people you talk to online.

Boyfriends and girlfriends

You may have very close friendships with people of the other sex, without having any romantic feelings towards them. You may just be good friends and feel comfortable talking to each other about all sorts of things. These types of friendships can be good, because you have the opportunity to discuss issues openly and honestly with someone of the other sex, without the involvement of a relationship.

When you start to have romantic or sexual feelings towards another person, there is no reason why you can't still enjoy the same type of friendship as before. However, many young people start to feel shy and awkward with people they are attracted to. The best way to get to know someone is to try and relax and be yourself.

In the past there was the expectation for the boy to make the first move, and girls were expected to wait to be asked. These expectations of sex roles sometimes put restrictions on how people behaved. These days it is becoming more acceptable for the girl to do the asking, and young people generally find this OK.

Everyone feels embarrassed at some time in their life.

Same-sex attractions

During early adolescence it is quite common for young people to have strong feelings for people of the same sex. It could be a friend, someone about your age that you don't know very well or someone older, like a teacher or a friend of your parents or older brother or sister. You might like this person because they are especially kind to you, because they are attractive or for no particular reason. These feelings are absolutely normal and it will have no bearing on whether you are heterosexual or homosexual when you grow up.

Often these types of feelings happen just when you are starting to have sexual thoughts and feelings. It may be that this is just one way of focusing your changing feelings, without the involvement of a relationship. This would also explain why you may have very strong crushes on a pop singer or a movie star.

When I try to talk to a girl I don't make any sense. — boy, 13 years

Everyone feels embarrassed at some time in their life, especially if they are trying to make new friends or impress someone. Try to talk about things you are interested in, and ask her about the things she likes. Listening and being interested in other people makes you a more interesting person. The important thing to remember is to relax and be yourself. Remember, you don't need to be talking all the time to be good company. Sometimes quiet times can be very special.

How do you ask a girl on a date? — boy, 11 years

The best way is to be honest and say you would like to go out with her and arrange to do something that you both like. Maybe go to a movie or to a fast-food place for lunch. If you are at a school dance or party, perhaps you could just start talking. This way you don't have to work up the courage to actually ask her out. Sometimes it is easier to ask a girl out with a group of friends. This is often a good way to get to know people a little better before just the two of you go out together.

My friend really likes a boy in our class. She doesn't know how to tell him. What should she do? — *girl, 14 years*

This is perfectly normal and can result in quite strong feelings. Sometimes these feelings can turn out to be very temporary or they can last for longer. Probably the best thing to do when you really like someone is to get to know them a bit better before letting them know how you feel. She could perhaps just start talking to him and arrange to do something together and find out if they get on OK. For some people part of the attraction is that the person is out of reach. Once the person shows some interest, feelings might change.

How can you confess you love someone without getting teased? — *boy, 10 years*

As people get older, their feelings towards other people often change and they may have very strong feelings towards another person. Your other friends may not have got to this stage and may not understand how you feel. When people do not understand something, they often handle this by teasing others. It is often a way of covering their own confusion.

It may be better to talk to the person privately. A good way to get to know someone better is by

Having a crush on someone is perfectly normal.

talking about the things you both are interested in or perhaps doing things together like playing sport or doing homework. If you are not sure the person you care about feels the same way, perhaps you should wait until you are a little more confident.

How can I tell my parents that I have a boyfriend?
— *girl, 13 years*

It's always a good idea to be honest with your parents. Some parents take a little while to get used to their children growing up and developing new relationships. Sometimes parents may think that their children are too young to have relationships with members of the other sex. They might feel that you are too young to become too involved with someone.

Maybe you can tell them that you really like this person and you enjoy spending time with him. They might feel more comfortable if you have contact with other people and go out with a group of people. Also, parents usually will feel more comfortable if you make it very clear, when you go out, where you are going and when you'll be home. If you stick to those arrangements they will trust you next time.

Is it OK to go out with a guy who is six years older than you? — *girl, 13 years*

If you are 13, a boy who is 19 is probably a little too old. This, of course, will depend on how mature both people are, but a 13-year-old and a 19-year-old would generally be interested in different things. This age difference may not be a problem for older people, but a 19-year-old may want a different type of relationship from a 13-year-old. For example, he may wish to drink alcohol at parties or hotels (and if he is over 18 he is legally able to), or he may want to stay out a lot later than a 13-year-old is allowed to or he might want to start a more serious or long-term relationship.

Such an age difference could also mean that there would be quite different expectations when it came to sex. Many young men of 19 are sexually active. Most people would agree that 13 is really too young to start having sex, and this is why the age of consent is 16. A 19-year-old who has sex with a 13-year-old would be breaking the law.

How do you get a boy to like you? — *girl, 11 years*
It's difficult to force someone to like you. If you really like someone, the best thing to do is to just try and be yourself. Get to know him by talking to him about things you are interested in, and ask him about his interests.

For you to think about

And perhaps discuss with a parent or an adult who cares about you

Try and put yourself in your parents' position and think about some of the things they may be worrying about as you get older.
Some of their concerns might be:

- that you might get injured
- that you are not working hard enough at school
- that you may get hurt emotionally
- that you may be pressured into having sex
- that your friends are a bad influence on you
- that you are not going out with friends often enough

Discussing these concerns with your parents may reassure them.

Chapter 4

Feeling healthy and looking after yourself

As we have said, growing up isn't just a physical process. You start to become more independent from your parents and other adults and more able to make decisions for yourself. This is a very important part of changing from a child into an adult. Some of these decisions will be about ways to keep your body healthy. Mum or Dad can't choose your clothes, make your meals or rub sunscreen on your nose forever! They will probably still have quite a say for a while, but eventually all these decisions will be up to you.

This chapter looks at some of the things involved in keeping a healthy and happy body. No one expects you to make healthy decisions all the time. The odd piece of chocolate, pig-out on pizza or couch-potato day doesn't hurt anyone — as long as it's not a way of life!

Having a healthy diet

Being hungry is a normal part of puberty. You need enough food to supply you with the energy needed to keep up with your rapid growth and busy life. Many parents complain about the huge amounts of food their adolescent children eat, and the fact that the fridge door is constantly open. An increased appetite is quite normal. It may be more noticeable in boys because they tend to grow so much. But girls will also experience a greater appetite.

Some girls may become quite self-conscious about the changing shape of their bodies. During the years leading up to and around the start of periods it is normal to increase your weight to prepare for periods. This may be quite a few kilograms. Unfortunately, dieting to try to reduce these normal fat deposits is very common for many young women. Often it is quite unnecessary, and sometimes it can be harmful.

Good eating habits start early, so it's important to learn how to maintain a balanced diet from an early age. Maintaining a well-balanced diet will also mean your body will grow in the best possible way.

What to drink

Try to drink at least eight glasses of fluid per day, and more if it's very hot or you're exercising a lot. Water is best and it contains no calories. Water helps to remove waste products from the body and helps prevent

Did you know?

About healthy eating

There are five food groups necessary to have a healthy diet. These are recommended daily food amounts in each group for young people.

Group 1   Vegetables and legumes
           Eat at least five servings
           One serve equals one cup of green leafy vegetables, half a potato or half a cup of corn, canned beans or lentils

Group 2   Fruit
           Eat two servings
           One serve equals one medium apple, orange or pear, two small apricots, one cup of canned fruit

Group 3   Grains (cereal foods, mostly wholegrain)
           Eat four to five servings
           One serve equals one slice of bread, a medium bread roll or wrap, half a cup of cooked rice, pasta, noodles, cooked porridge, a third of a cup of wheat cereal

Group 4   Lean meat and chicken, fish, eggs, tofu, nuts and seeds

Eat two and a half servings
One serve equals 65 grams of lean cooked meat, 80 grams of lean chicken, 100 grams of fish, two eggs, 170 grams of tofu

Group 5   Milk, yoghurt, cheese
Eat two to three servings
One serve equals one cup of milk, 40 grams of cheese, three quarters of a cup of yoghurt, one cup of soy or rice milk

Oils, spreads, nuts and seeds can be included in small quantities.

constipation. Keep soft drinks for special occasions. They're full of sugar and have no nutritional value.

Skipping meals

Skipping meals won't help you lose weight. Most people who miss a meal catch up by snacking on less healthy food throughout the day. The most commonly missed meal is breakfast, probably because we all like to sleep in! Having a healthy breakfast helps with concentration at school and work. One study has found that people who regularly ate breakfast actually lived longer.

If you are in a rush in the morning, try eating a good-sized bowl of cereal that is low in sugar, or a tub of yoghurt with a piece of fruit or two. If you do have to eat on the run, how about a banana sandwich using wholemeal bread, or a crispbread with cottage cheese and sultanas — and grab a glass of milk before you go. Have a look through any cookbooks or magazines that you have at home, then use your imagination and create different foods that suit your taste.

Snacks

The healthiest snacks include fresh and dried fruit, raw vegetables, nuts (instead of potato chips), sandwiches, pitta bread or crispbreads. Biscuits, cakes and muesli bars are all high in sugar, so should be eaten only now and then.

Being a vegetarian

A balanced vegetarian diet can be a very healthy diet. It should be low in fat and high in foods such as fruit, vegetables and carbohydrates. However, achieving a balanced vegetarian diet requires a lot of planning to ensure adequate iron, calcium, zinc and B vitamins. Some people choose a vegan diet, which is a type of vegetarian diet. Vegans only eat plant-based foods and do not eat any food that comes from animals, such as meat, fish, eggs, milk, yoghurt and cheese. People may choose a vegan diet because of their religion, concern for the environment or animal rights.

Before deciding to follow any diet that excludes nutritious food groups, it is a good idea to see a dietitian. It can be difficult to get the right balance of food to stay healthy.

The facts about fast food

Most fast foods are very high in fat, salt and sugar, and this means that they are very high in calories. In fact one fast-food-chain meal of a large burger, large fries, milkshake and sundae would contain the recommended daily calories for some people. Fast food is convenient, it tastes good and it's OK to eat it occasionally. But try not to eat out every day, and when you do, make sure that the rest of your food for that day is extra healthy.

At what age do you go on a diet? — *girl, 13 years*
Most young people need never go on a diet. Our bodies need a certain amount of fat to be healthy. Most young people who think they are overweight are in fact quite healthy, and sometimes even underweight for their height.

If a person of any age is extremely overweight or obese, he or she should be guided by a

Most young people need never go on a diet.

Did you know?

About eating disorders

Anorexia nervosa

Anorexia nervosa is an illness that mainly affects girls, although boys can suffer from it as well. Those suffering from anorexia nervosa have a distorted view of their body, believing that they are or will become fat. This leads to the person eating less and less in the hope of losing weight that isn't there.

Bulimia

Similarly, people with bulimia have an extreme fear of gaining weight. Instead of not eating, the bulimic person will binge or eat huge amounts and then get rid of the food by vomiting or taking laxatives. They believe that this way they will not gain weight.

Having an eating disorder is a very serious health problem. Those who suffer may be severely depressed and may require treatment for quite a long time. Their growth and development may be affected and, if severe, can damage important organs of the body or even lead to death from malnutrition.

Symptoms and signs may include:
- Extreme loss of weight
- Always counting calories

- Being preoccupied with dieting and exercise
- Frequent weighing
- Not menstruating regularly or periods stopping
- Unexplained vomiting
- Being ashamed or defensive about eating

There are specialist doctors and clinics for people with eating disorders. If you suspect that you or someone you know has an eating disorder, it is important that you speak to an adult you trust who can assist you. Treatment can be very successful, but may involve long-term management for the individual and his or her family.

doctor or dietitian as to how to lose weight. Being obese is a health problem. For people who are just a little overweight, simply cutting out foods in between meals and avoiding sweet drinks such as soft drink and juice should be enough. If you are hungry between meals, have a piece of fruit or a raw vegetable, such as a carrot or a celery stick.

If you think you are overweight, talk with Mum or Dad or another caring adult before you start to diet.

Body image

We all have a mental image of how we would like our body to look. Often it is very different from the body we have. If we asked a group of 13-year-olds if they could change anything about their body what would it be, nearly everyone would have a list of wants. Perhaps it would be a slimmer or taller body, bigger muscles, a better tan, a smaller nose, whiter teeth or different coloured hair. It would be a rare teenager who would be completely happy with her or his looks and wouldn't change a thing.

How do we form this ideal body type in our minds? These attitudes and beliefs are learnt from images all around us — on TV, in movies, in magazines and newspapers, and from the beliefs held by the people we admire and like.

In the past and in many cultures today, the idea of a beautiful woman is one who is well rounded and soft. Look in any art book — that was how the popular models looked. In many cultures being thin is a sign of poor health and poverty.

Unfortunately, the body ideal that is projected by models and female actors today is not the ideal healthy body type. Physically, women's bodies should have broad hips and some fat on their stomach, hips and thighs. This provides the best body type for general health and for pregnancy and childbirth. Women who are very underweight can actually stop menstruating. Of course, some women will have a very slim body shape regardless of how much they eat, and this is normal for them.

Just as there is a lot of pressure on girls to look like the models in magazines, there can be similar pressure on boys or young men to look like Superman clones, with extremely lean and muscular bodies.

The male and female models we see on TV and in magazines spend their whole lives ensuring that they are slim or muscular. This means that most of them would be constantly dieting and exercising. Some of them even have personal trainers to manage their diet and exercise plan! This is totally unrealistic for most people. Pictures in magazines have been touched up with tints and airbrushes, covering up spots or pimples, giving bluer eyes, painting in a perfect tan or 'trimming off' a largish nose or chin. Make-up artists and hair stylists spend hours perfecting the model's looks.

The way you look will largely be determined by your genes, that is, what you've inherited from your mum and dad. Exercise and diet will also play a part, but your basic body shape and type are impossible to change. And why should you anyway? The way you look is fine, because it is you. Don't try to look like the Hollywood ideal. No one really looks like Ken and Barbie, and who would want to? Be proud of yourself and like who you are, then other people will like you too.

Is it all right to try to get the perfect body?
— *girl, 13 years*
A perfect body is a body that is healthy. This means that it is neither overweight nor underweight, but within the normal range for age and height. It should have a reasonable amount of muscle tone, and skin

should not be overexposed to the sun. This sort of body is easily obtained by most people. If a person is constantly dieting, exercising or sunbaking to achieve a 'perfect body', he or she has a totally unrealistic and probably unattainable body image. Having regular and enjoyable exercise, plenty of fresh air and a balanced diet should be all it takes.

Why do girls always go on diets?
— boy, 13 years

Girls often go on diets because they believe they are overweight. This is rarely the case. Most are quite healthy just the way they are. Some boys and girls will put on quite a lot of weight early in puberty. As your body develops, this extra weight will not be as noticeable. Rather than going on a diet, just eat sensibly.

My mum says I am too young to wear make-up. What can I do to make her change her mind?
— girl, 13 years

Many women grew up when it wasn't fashionable to wear a lot of make-up. Girls who did may have been seen as being a bit 'wild'. So for some women of this generation it is difficult for them to accept wearing make-up as a usual practice. Wearing make-up is also a sign of growing up, and sometimes this is hard for parents to accept. Your mum might want to keep you a 'little girl' for a while longer.

If your parents don't want you to wear make-up, but you do, try talking about it with them. Pick a time

For you to think about

Most of us spend a lot of time thinking about the things we don't like about our bodies. It may be better for us to concentrate on what we do like. Stand in front of the mirror and try to list all your good features. Perhaps you like your eyes or hair. You may have good skin or nice hands or teeth. Keep these features in your mind and make the most of them.

when they are not too busy or stressed, and try not to get angry or annoyed. Tell them how you are feeling. Perhaps that you are feeling left out because your friends are all wearing make-up, or that you want to appear a little more grown up.

Be prepared to compromise. You may be able to agree on just wearing make-up for very special occasions, or just a little bit to start with, like a touch of mascara and lipstick. If they do agree, don't overdo it by wearing lots, otherwise they might change their minds.

How do I get bigger muscles? — *boy, 12 years*
Once you go through puberty, exercise will help to develop muscles. If you do exercise with weights, this may also help. Young people need to be careful with weights while their bodies are developing. It's a good idea to have a talk with a qualified gym instructor before you start.

Regular exercise will help to keep you healthy and your body looking its best. But if you have a slight frame, no amount of weightlifting or exercise will change it into Mr Universe. Be happy with the body type that you have. It belongs to you and that should be special enough!

How come some girls have bigger breasts than others? — *girl, 12 years*

Breast size is another characteristic inherited from our parents. Some girls' breasts will grow bigger than others'. There is nothing you can do to make your breasts bigger or smaller. Exercise can reduce the amount of body fat you have, but it won't change your breast size dramatically.

Is it true that most girls are self-conscious about the size of their breasts? — *girl, 14 years*

Some girls are self-conscious about the size of their breasts. If a girl has large breasts she may wish she had smaller ones, and if they are small she may wish them bigger. People often wish for the unattainable. We should all try to be happy with what we have.

Why do some women get breast implants? — *girl, 12 years*

Some women are not happy with the way they look, and think that making their breasts larger will make them happy. This is not surprising as we are constantly bombarded with media and advertising

Did you know?

About wearing make-up

- Make-up has been used in many societies for more than 5000 years. It is just one way of modifying or changing how people look. The wearing of wigs, fancy clothes and jewellery, nail polish and perfume have all been fashionable over the years. More permanent forms of body decoration include tattoos or piercing parts of the body to wear earrings or nose ornaments of all shapes and sizes. Some tribal communities decorate the body with skin scarring, stretching lips and earlobes and body painting.
- Make-up has been worn in the past for many different reasons including to indicate social class, status or gender, to disguise or protect from the sun, or to make the wearer look younger, healthier or more beautiful.
- Ancient Egyptians based their make-up on hydrosilicate of copper, which acted as a form of sunscreen lotion. This eventually led to the use of make-up for decorative purposes. Cleopatra and other upper-class Egyptian women would spend many hours painting their eyelids and eyebrows. They even had special cushions to rest their elbows on to steady their hands.
- Cosmetics have also been used to cover damaged skin, scars caused by illness, even

blemishes caused by the harsh chemicals in make-up used before. This explains the fashion of wearing beauty spots and patches in the seventeenth century.

- Today, modern make-up is safe and hygienic, and its quality allows it to be used in smaller amounts to greater effect. Its use is dictated by fashion and this changes regularly, but generally 'the look' is to emphasise eyes, making them look larger; to tone the skin, giving it a smooth and healthy appearance; and to outline and colour the lips so that they look full and well-shaped.

- You don't have to wear make-up unless you want to, and you shouldn't feel pressured by your friends to do so. Remember, wearing make-up is just another fashion to follow. You can appear attractive and healthy just by keeping your skin and hair clean and a smile on your face!

- If you do choose to use make-up, one way to learn how to apply it properly is to visit the cosmetic departments of the larger stores. Most of these shops offer free demonstrations. They will probably try to sell you their brand, but you are not under any obligation, so only buy if you really want the products and only if you can afford them. Most cosmetic brands have very similar ingredients and quality. The less expensive ones available from most supermarkets are much the same as those with a fancy, up-market label.

that tells us how we should look or act. It is important to remember that feeling happy about ourselves or having good self-esteem is about feeling good on the inside, not about how we look on the outside.

Cosmetic surgery

Cosmetic surgery is surgery that alters a person's face or body. Breast enlargement is one of the most common types. Cosmetic surgery also includes other procedures such as making the breasts smaller, facelifts and changing the shape of the body.

People may have cosmetic surgery because they want to look younger or they want to change a feature they do not like.

If a person decides to have cosmetic surgery it is important for them to think about it carefully, understand the risks of the procedure and be realistic about the results. They need to be sure that they are having it done for themselves and are not being pressured by someone else. Cosmetic surgery won't solve personal problems but may help a person feel more self-confident.

Exercise

Exercise in the past was a way of life. There weren't cars to drive children to school, so people had to walk or ride a bike or horse. There were no computer games, TVs, smart phones or movie theatres, so children had to

Did you know?

About exercise

Regular physical activity is important for people of all ages for lots of reasons:

- increasing strength and muscle tone
- keeping the body well-toned by burning up extra kilojoules
- improving physical endurance, so a person can do more without getting tired
- improving the body's circulation, so all of the muscles and organs in the body work well together
- keeping joints loose and supple and helping to prevent stiffness and soreness
- improving posture
- increasing the ability to concentrate and having faster reaction time
- helping people cope with stress
- increasing energy
- providing more restful sleep
- increasing self-esteem and self-confidence

make their own fun, often outdoors with lots of other neighbourhood children and pets. Housework was all done by hand, not with washing machines, dryers, vacuum cleaners and dishwashers, and most children helped with these chores. All of these activities required lots of energy and helped to keep people fit and healthy.

Gradually life has become less active. This means we sit on our bottoms a lot more than we used to.

Keeping all of this in mind, exercise should be enjoyable and never painful. The old saying 'no pain, no gain' is not necessarily true. Choose activities that are fun — dancing, riding your bike, swimming or surfing, walking your dog or baby brother or sister, skipping, tennis or playing team games such as netball, soccer or baseball. Set your own pace and don't continue if you find yourself becoming very tired or if your body starts to hurt.

If you haven't been exercising much, increase the amount very gradually. Start with about 15 minutes and build up comfortably. The recommended amount is about 15–20 minutes of continuous activity between three and five times per week. Start with a warm-up period and finish with a slower cooling-down time, and drink plenty of water to replace the fluids you lose when you exercise.

If you do play team or competitive sport, remember why you are playing — for fun, for exercise and as a social activity. Winning is exciting and rewarding, but it isn't the only reason people play. Sometimes people can push themselves too hard; this can lead to disappointment and often to injury. If you are unwell or injured you shouldn't play, and others should admire you for being sensible. In the long run you will perform better.

My mum says I shouldn't wear bike pants under my sports uniform. Why not?
— girl, 12 years
Most bike pants are made of lycra, which is a synthetic material. Synthetic materials do not allow as much circulation of air as natural fibres like cotton. The genitals contain lots of sweat glands, and as you play sport your pants will become quite moist with sweat. Synthetics against the skin will keep the moisture in, and that could lead to irritations, or a common fungal infection called thrush. Cotton pants will absorb any sweat and help to keep the genitals dry and healthy.

Recreation

As well as regular exercise, it is important to leave time for more restful recreation with your family, your friends or just by yourself. Recreation other than exercise might include reading, painting, playing on the computer, playing board or card games, going on picnics or to the movies or simply sitting with people you care about and talking.

Watching television is another form of restful recreation; however, it tends to be fairly antisocial. When people sit down and watch TV together, their eyes and minds are glued to the TV and not to each other. TV rarely stretches the imagination or creativity either, so try to limit the amount of TV you watch to shows that you are really interested in, instead of watching whatever is on.

Sleep

Growing requires lots of energy, and sleep helps your body recover at the end of the day. Many adolescents find that they actually need more sleep than they used to. Adequate sleep is important for physical and emotional health. The amount of sleep each individual requires varies, but most 10- to 14-year-olds need about 10 hours' sleep. Your body is the best judge. If you wake up after eight hours feeling fresh and energetic, that is probably enough for you. If you find it hard to get up in time for school, try going to bed a little earlier. Some people find they need a lot more sleep than others.

Hygiene or keeping clean

Why would you have to wash more frequently at puberty? — *girl, 10 years*
All people, no matter what age they are, need to keep themselves clean. During puberty your body

Did you know?

About keeping the genitals clean

A white substance called smegma is secreted from the glands around the end of a boy's penis. The smegma should be washed away each day, or it can become smelly and lead to an infection. If a boy has not been circumcised, he will need to draw back his foreskin and wash around the end of his penis. If the foreskin doesn't pull back easily, he shouldn't force it. Sometimes it requires some gentle stretching, and rarely will it require circumcision. Both of these options should be discussed with a doctor if necessary.

Smegma is also secreted from the glands around the female's clitoris. Girls should wash their genitals carefully at least once a day, making sure that they wash gently in between the folds of skin. This will wash away any stale smegma and vaginal mucus.

It is not necessary to wash the genital area with lots of soap. Never use perfumed sprays around the genitals, as they are too harsh. A mild, unperfumed soap and plenty of water is all that is necessary. Sometimes even a mild soap can be irritating, especially to sensitive skin. If this is the case, just stick to lots of warm water.

Wiping front to back

Girls should wipe their vulva with toilet paper after urinating. Care should be taken to wipe from the front to the back. This is to make sure that no germs or bacteria that live in the bowel are transferred to the vagina or urethra, where they could cause an infection.

will start to produce much more oil (called sebum) and you'll start to sweat more. If sweat and sebum are not washed off regularly, your body will smell. Regular washing also washes away the daily dirt that all people accumulate.

Circumcision

Is it important for a male baby to be circumcised?
— boy, 12 years

Circumcision is an operation in which the foreskin (the loose skin that covers the tip of the penis) is removed. A very small percentage of boys will need to be circumcised because their foreskin is too tight and can't be pulled back by mid-childhood. Apart from these boys there is no medical reason for circumcision.

In some cultures circumcision is performed for religious reasons.

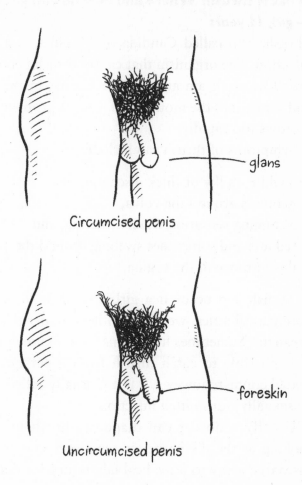

Circumcised penis

glans

Uncircumcised penis

foreskin

In the past, people believed it was more hygienic to be circumcised, but as long as a boy pulls back his foreskin and washes his penis each day it will stay quite clean. Otherwise, smegma can build up and cause an infection. In some cultures circumcision is performed for religious reasons.

What is thrush? Where and how do you get it?
— girl, 14 years

Thrush, also called Candida or Monillia, is a fungal infection. The organism that causes thrush is normally found in small amounts in the vagina, in the bowel and sometimes the mouth, and is not a problem unless it grows too rapidly.

Symptoms of thrush can include:

- a white, milky or thick discharge,
- itchiness around the vulva,
- a stinging sensation when urinating, and
- redness and sometimes swelling around the vulva or the entrance to the vagina.

Thrush can occur if a girl is tired or ill, if she is taking antibiotics, wearing synthetic underpants or is pregnant. Sometimes it happens for no known reason. It is possible to catch thrush from a person during sexual contact; however, it is not usually called an STI, or sexually transmitted infection.

Usually a doctor can diagnose thrush by simply looking at the discharge, or sending a sample of the discharge away to a medical laboratory for diagnosis. It is easily treated with cream or tablets.

Sometimes the tops of my legs get red and itchy, especially after playing football. Why?
— boy, 14 years

When you are very active or playing sport, you will sweat more, and this can cause a local skin irritation.

Did you know?

About vaginal discharge

All women have vaginal discharge. It consists of fluid that drains from the uterus, secretions from the cervix and fluids that keep the vagina moist, lubricated and clean. It may be clear, white or very pale yellow, but it may dry darker on underpants. The amount and colour varies depending on the menstrual cycle. At the time of ovulation, about mid-cycle, the mucus is usually clear and stretchy, like the white of an uncooked egg.

The smell is usually mild, particularly if the girl washes regularly. If the smell changes or becomes unpleasant, it may be a good idea to see a doctor, just to check that an infection hasn't developed.

This can happen around the top of your legs, in your groin, under your arms or sometimes around your stomach. It's important to have a shower as soon as possible after playing sport. Dry yourself well and perhaps use a little unperfumed talcum powder. If the rash continues to be a problem, you may need to get some cream or a special powder from the chemist. Make sure that you wear clean clothes every time you play sport.

Do you have to use a deodorant after puberty?
— *girl, 11 years*

Everyone sweats; it's the body's way of cooling down. The armpits contain numerous sweat glands and as sweating increases at puberty, this is a time that many people start to wear a deodorant. Young people are so active that they may sweat quite a lot. If sweat dries and becomes old it will become smelly, but washing each day and after strenuous sport or physical activity will prevent that happening. Many people find that wearing a deodorant helps to prevent body odour.

Deodorants help to prevent the smell that develops from sweating. Fresh sweat doesn't have an unpleasant smell, but as the day wears on it may become stale and smell. Wearing a deodorant is a personal choice, but keep in mind you will probably smell a lot fresher if you do.

When should you start shaving your legs?
— *girl, 11 years*

There is no particular time to start shaving or waxing your legs. In fact, many women never shave or wax their legs because they feel it is not necessary, and it is

Did you know?

About pimples and blackheads

- Pimples occur when a duct or pore of the skin becomes blocked. At puberty, the amount of oil or sebum your skin produces increases because it is stimulated by one of the hormones released at puberty. If the pores become blocked, sebum builds up and forms pimples.
- Most people will get pimples at some stage in their life. It is more common at puberty, but can happen at any time.
- Blackheads are not dirt. They are caused by plugs of sebum on the surface of the skin. When sebum is exposed to air its colour darkens.
- Whiteheads are caused when a small amount of pus comes to the top of the blockage.
- Using heavy moisturisers and some sunscreen lotions may also cause the pores to block up and pimples to form.
- Chocolate and fatty foods don't usually cause pimples or acne, but having a healthy diet will help keep your skin (and the rest of your body) healthy.
- A little sunlight can help pimples, but too much can actually make the skin more inflamed.

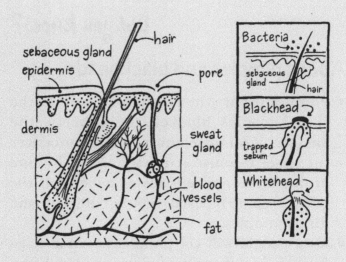

- Treatment includes keeping the face clean. Using mild soap with warm water twice a day is usually enough; try this before you spend any money on special cleansers. Creams available from the chemist can be applied to pimples, to help dry them out.
- Facial scrubs, harsh rubbing, or steam treatments can make pimples worse, because they may stimulate oil production.
- Some girls notice a break-out of pimples just before or during their period. This is due to the change in hormones that occurs as part of their normal menstrual cycle.
- Severe pimples or acne should be checked by a doctor, and may need specialist treatment. This may include antibiotics or other medications.

more natural to leave them as they are. It is a personal choice, and it is important to have a think about it and decide how you want to look. Don't feel you have to do it just because others are doing it. It's also a good idea to talk to your mum, your dad or someone you trust before you decide.

Pubic shaving

As well as shaving under their arms and legs, some people shave part or all of their pubic hair. They may do it because they think it is more hygienic and more attractive. While we don't really know why humans have pubic hair, it is a natural part of our body and it is important that it is the person's own choice and they shouldn't feel pressured to shave any part of their body if they don't want to.

Tattoos

People get tattoos for a number of reasons. It may be a way to express themselves, a reminder of a special person or event, to identify with a particular group or for cultural reasons. Many indigenous people around the world have applied tattoos for centuries. These may help identify which tribal or family group a person belongs to. They might also be a mark of status, or celebrate the end of childhood and the beginning of adulthood. Some indigenous cultures use scars on their bodies for the same reasons.

If a person decides to get a tattoo when they are older, it is important for them to think it through as tattoos are intended to be permanent. If a person changes their mind later, the tattoo may be difficult to remove without scarring and pain. Getting a tattoo has some risks such as infection, allergy and scarring.

In most countries you have to be over 18 to get a tattoo, unless you have consent from your parents.

Immunisation

Just like the immunisations you had when you were a baby to protect you against diseases such as measles, there is a vaccine to protect you from HPV (human papillomavirus). HPV is a virus that can cause cancer. In Ireland the vaccine is offered to girls in first year of second-level school through the school-based Human Papillomavirus (HPV) Vaccination Program.

This free vaccine is given as two injections over a period of six months. It is important to complete the full course for the best protection. A female who has had the immunisation will still need to have regular Pap smears once she starts having sexual intercourse.

Teeth

Everyone who has reached puberty will already be cleaning her or his teeth two or three times a day. This helps prevent tooth decay, and keeps the gums healthy. Cleaning teeth also freshens your breath, and we all know that there is nothing worse than talking to someone with smelly breath. Using dental floss also helps to keep teeth and gums healthy. Dental floss is waxed or unwaxed thread that is pulled in between the teeth to remove any pieces of food caught there. Ask one of your parents to show you how to use it, or ask the dentist next time you have an appointment.

Protecting yourself from the sun

The image of suntanned bodies as healthy is outdated and dangerous. We now know that there is no such thing as 'a healthy tan'. Tanned skin is sun-damaged skin. The most serious consequence of sun damage is skin cancer. However, skin cancer is only one result of too much sun. Wrinkles, dry or rough skin and uneven skin colour or blotchiness are all caused by exposure to the sun. To keep your skin looking healthy, it's best to follow a few simple rules:

- Try to stay out of the sun during the hottest part of the day. This is usually between about 10 a.m. and 2 p.m. If you are holidaying at the beach, why not have an early swim in the morning and then perhaps a little more time on the beach in the late afternoon?
- Whenever you are in the sun, wear a hat and SPF 30+ sunscreen. Cover your skin by wearing a T-shirt or long-sleeved shirt — even when you're swimming, if you can. Reapply sunscreen regularly,

particularly if you are sweating a lot, or swimming. Make sure you try out your sunscreen before you play sport. Some brands may irritate your eyes if you sweat a lot. Some are promoted for use when playing sport. If you are unsure, ask the chemist. Some make-up has built-in sun protection and this will be indicated on the label.

• A little bit of sunlight is healthy, but this doesn't mean lying in the sun for long periods.

By being sensible all year round and not just in summer, you will keep your skin in the best possible condition. Don't be fooled by a crazy fashion. Make your own fashion statement and stick with a healthy complexion.

Smoking

Everyone knows that smoking is bad for you. It causes lung disease, heart disease and cancer. Many more people die from smoking-related diseases than from car accidents. Unfortunately, while the general rate of smoking is decreasing, the number of young people smoking is actually increasing.

Young people are more likely to smoke if they:

- have friends or family who smoke,
- find it difficult to say 'no', especially to their friends or people they are trying to impress,
- are unaware of the health risks,
- don't feel good about themselves in general, or
- find it difficult to cope with stress.

Some people smoke to look cool or to impress other people, but a person who hates the smell and the look of smoking won't be impressed at all. A person is more likely to impress others by feeling confident and being themselves. Smoking turns teeth and fingers yellow and causes bad breath; just try smelling a full ashtray!

Remember, *you* are in charge of your body, so make your own decisions and be proud of them. Smoking is an expensive habit that is hard to break once started. Think of all the other things that you could be spending your money on.

Remember, *you* are in charge of your body.

Alcohol

It is illegal to drink alcohol if you are under the age of 18, but some young people may drink before this. Perhaps they start to drink to make themselves appear more grown up. Drinking alcohol in large amounts will kill off brain cells, may make you vomit (imagine how that would look), and will affect your ability to make good decisions and judgments.

This includes decisions about whether or not to have sex. Drinking alcohol can make people more likely to say 'yes' to sex, when normally they would say 'no'. When this happens, the person will often regret the experience and feel guilty later. Also, young people who have sex when they are drunk are less likely to use contraception or practise safe sex. Unplanned pregnancy could result, or a sexually transmitted infection could be passed on.

If you do choose to drink, whatever age you are, it is important that you drink in moderation, and never so much that you don't know what you are doing. Drinking alcohol and driving, in particular, is potentially very dangerous.

Other drugs

Abuse of any kind of drug or medicine is dangerous. It can damage your brain as well as other parts of your body, and abuse may lead to addiction — which means great difficulty in giving up even if you want to. Your judgment may be affected while you are under the influence of some drugs and you may do things that you normally wouldn't want to, or that are dangerous.

Why do some people take drugs?
— boy, 12 years

There is no one reason why a person takes drugs. It could be just to experiment to see what it is like. Perhaps it is due to peer pressure. Some people take drugs to help cope with pressure, to relieve boredom, or to rebel against or reject their parents. If you are worried about drug abuse you should talk with a responsible adult whom you trust, or ring a drug and alcohol support agency. You can find these agencies online.

For you to think about

Think about what you would say if someone you liked offered you:

- cigarettes
- drugs
- alcoholic drinks

Practise in front of the mirror, or with a parent or grown-up. What would you say? How could you respond if the person started teasing or laughing at you? This is a good way for you to rehearse for a real situation.

Chapter 5

Looking after your mental health

W hen people talk about mental health, they mean how you think and feel about things. Feeling mentally healthy is about being able to handle things that are going on in your life. It is about being able to manage the changes and cope with all the things that happen to you, both good and bad. It is about being aware of your thoughts and feelings, whether they are positive or negative. These feelings might include happiness, sadness, joy and despair.

Being mentally healthy is also about making and keeping relationships with other people. The types of relationships people have will vary depending on their situation, but will probably include relationships with parents, family, friends or teachers.

You probably already know many of the terms that are used to describe mental health, such as 'self-esteem', 'body image', 'mood swings', 'anxiety' and 'depression'. This chapter looks at some of these terms to help you understand what mental health is all about and how they relate to you.

Self-esteem

You may have heard people talk about self-esteem, and how some people have high self-esteem and how others have low self-esteem. It is a term that is used a lot but what does it mean?

Self-esteem is about how people value themselves. People with high self-esteem mostly feel good about things; they are confident and believe in themselves. They may have days when they experience some self-doubt, but generally they feel that they are worthwhile. People with low self-esteem, on the other hand, nearly always have self-doubt and don't value themselves. They lack confidence and are always comparing themselves to others and feeling they don't measure up, which is a sure way for anyone to feel inadequate.

There are lots of things that contribute to how you feel about yourself, including your personal circumstances and the experiences you have had. Even though you don't always have control over these events, there are some ways you can help yourself to feel better about things and improve your self-esteem.

Did you know?

Ways to improve your self-esteem

- Stop giving yourself a hard time — don't always compare yourself to others
- Focus on the things you *can do* rather than what you can't do — think about all those times you have been successful
- Start talking to yourself in a positive way — this is called positive self-talk. You can do this by telling yourself a positive statement every day. For example, you may tell yourself how well you achieved something during the day, or you may simply tell yourself that you are OK, or you believe that today things will be OK, no matter what happens
- Set yourself some realistic goals. Start by setting small goals and gradually work up to bigger things. For example, if you want to learn to play the guitar you could aim to learn a new chord each week
- Learn a new skill
- Compliment someone on how they look or on something they have done well — it is amazing how good you can feel when you make someone else feel good!
- See mistakes as an opportunity to learn

- Think about other people rather than yourself. Caring about others is a great way to forget feeling sad about yourself
- Focus on relationships that are positive and important to you
- Talk to someone about how you are feeling
- Do some exercise or an activity you enjoy
- Make a list of all the things that make you happy!

Body image

Body image is the term used to describe the way people think they look. It's how people feel about their body size and shape. Even though it is a fact that people come in all shapes and sizes, some people may have unrealistic ideas about their bodies and think they are too fat, too thin, too tall or too short etc. Most people want to be accepted by others, and that includes being accepted for the way they look. This may be more of an issue for you at puberty when your body is changing a lot. For example, perhaps you are going through puberty later than your friends and feel different from everyone else.

People are constantly getting messages about how they should look and what sort of a person they should be. These messages may come from parents, friends, teachers, movies, television and magazines. It can be pretty exhausting and disheartening trying to live up to these expectations. Some people begin to feel depressed about the way they look, and in some cases develop eating disorders such as anorexia nervosa or bulimia. These are discussed in Chapter 4.

Try to think about the pressures you are feeling to look or dress a certain way. Where is the pressure coming from? Is it from family or friends or the media? Remember, most of the images in the media are there to sell you something, so they use models that make the products (such as clothes, shoes, shampoo etc) look as good as possible. How many REAL people do you know who look like the models in magazines or on television? Also remember that the media use all sorts of tricks to make the models look thinner and taller than they actually are.

Remember that while it may be important to look good, it is much more important to feel good.

If there is a particular part of your body you don't like, it's OK to acknowledge that you are not happy with it. If it is something you can't change, try and accept it as part of what makes you the unique person you are. Then focus on the parts of your body you do like.

Relationships

As discussed in Chapter 3, one of the significant changes that happens at puberty is the nature of the relationships you have with the people around you. These include relationships with your parents, family, friends and teachers. For example, as you mature you may want more independence from your parents and choose to spend more time with your friends.

Having positive relationships helps to keep you mentally healthy: you are more likely to feel better about yourself and better able to cope with things that happen to you.

The most difficult thing about relationships is that you don't have control of what the other person thinks or does. If relationships aren't going well it can be stressful and can affect the way you feel about yourself and life in general.

It is helpful if you are aware of how relationships affect you. You can do this by thinking about a particular relationship and how you feel when you are around that person; try to work out what is it about the relationship that makes you feel that way. Being aware of what is important to you in a relationship helps you to be in relationships that are positive. If you think the relationship isn't a healthy one, you need to find things you can do to remove yourself from that relationship.

In Chapter 3 there are some strategies to help you with the changing relationships you may experience as you go through puberty.

Did you know?

Things that make a healthy relationship

- **Honesty**—Being open and honest about what you think, and allowing the other person to be honest with you

- **Trust**—Being able to feel safe with each other

- **Respect**—Both being able to feel that you are listened to and valued, and that your opinions are respected

- **Loyalty**—Being able to rely on each other

- **Empathy**—Understanding each other

- **Forgiveness**—Not letting occasional spats get in the way of your friendships. Mood swings are common at puberty, and you or your friends may occasionally get out of sorts with each other or just want to be alone at times

While all relationships will have their ups and downs, healthy relationships should make you feel positive most of the time.

Shyness

While some people enjoy being alone at times, others feel lonely a lot of the time. This may be caused by shyness: they worry about not being liked or not fitting in and are afraid of being rejected by people. They may be giving themselves negative messages such as 'No-one will like me' or 'I'll make a fool of myself if I say something'. They feel left out of things.

If you are shy and find it difficult to talk to people, the first thing you need to do is to stop the negative feelings and start some positive self-talk. Think about one positive thing about yourself every day. It may seem weird at first, but if you persist it will become a habit.

It is also helpful to practise ways of starting a conversation. Listen to how others do it and then practise in front of a mirror or with your parents. Remember, you don't always have to do all the talking (in fact, this can get very boring for the other person). Asking questions and being a good listener is an important part of being a good communicator. To be an interesting person you need to be an *interested* person!

You could decide to join a group or start an activity where you will meet people who are interested in the same things as you. This way you will have something in common with the other members and have something to talk about. You will also be doing something you enjoy and hopefully be more relaxed about talking to people and getting to know them.

It is important to remember that all sorts of people can be shy, and the person you may consider to be unfriendly or 'snobby' may actually just be shy. You could help them by initiating conversation and asking them questions about what has been happening at school or what they did on the weekend. Nearly everyone responds well to being asked about themselves and being listened to. Even if you don't succeed at first, keep trying. It's really a case of nothing ventured, nothing gained.

Depression

Most people feel sad from time to time. It is a normal part of life. Being depressed can mean a number of things. It may mean that you are just feeling sad for a short while, or you may feel depressed because something traumatic has happened, such as someone you love has died or is very sick. Sadness or grief is a normal reaction to loss, and different people will react in different ways. You may feel anxious, angry or confused, and have trouble understanding what has happened, whereas some people may not seem affected at all. It may be hard to talk about how you feel. These are all normal responses. It can be very difficult but usually with time you will start to feel better; the time it takes will vary between different people.

When you are sad or miserable you may not feel like doing anything and just want to sit around watching

TV or spend time alone. You may believe that nothing interesting happens and you have no friends. Most of the time these feelings and moods do not last long and you are soon back to feeling your usual self.

Around puberty these moods may happen a bit more often. This is because you are developing emotionally and mentally as well as physically, which impacts on how you think about things and the way you relate to other people. Even though life may seem confusing or overwhelming at times, remember that growing up is a gradual process and it can take a little while to adjust. Try not to give yourself a hard time by being negative about yourself generally.

There are things that may help you feel better. Talking to someone often helps; this may be your parents, brother or sister, or friends. It also helps to do something you enjoy, or exercise. Exercise, like walking or bike riding, can distract you from your worries and lift your mood. It also improves sleep patterns. Getting enough sleep is very important to your mental health.

Depression is also a term used to describe a mental illness – this is when someone feels depressed most of the time. This is more serious and usually requires medical help.

If these sad feelings happen a lot of the time, or if you feel really bad or even feel like hurting yourself, it is important to tell someone you trust, or talk to a health professional. There are places that you can contact that have trained counsellors who you can talk to by phone and email, or through online counselling. They will talk things over or put you in contact with others who will be able to help.

If you are concerned about a friend who is depressed, you can help by listening to them, spending time with them, and encouraging them to talk to an adult or health professional. If they won't get help for themselves and you are concerned about them harming themselves, you will need to talk to an adult about it; even if your friend has made you promise not to tell anyone, it is better to do this than risk something bad happening. That would be worse.

Whether it is you or a friend who needs help, there are people you can talk to who will help you cope with whatever is happening.

Anxiety

Anxiety is a normal feeling that people have when they are faced with a situation that is potentially dangerous, difficult, stressful or embarrassing. Some examples could be making a presentation to your class, sitting exams, learning or doing something new, going to a party, starting a new school, or playing in a sporting competition. People can also have feelings of anxiety after something traumatic happens to them, such as being in an accident, or the death of someone close to them.

Feelings of anxiety may include sweaty palms, faster heart rate, 'butterflies' in the stomach, and shaky knees. Everyone is different — some people are natural worriers and seem to experience these symptoms of anxiety often, whereas others seem not to get too worried about anything at all.

You also may feel anxious because someone is putting pressure on you to do well at school or at sport. This pressure may come from parents or teachers. If this pressure is making you feel anxious or unhappy, it is good if you can tell someone. You may be able to talk to the person who is putting pressure on you — they may not realise what effect it is having on you. If you can't talk to them, it is good if you can tell someone else how you are feeling.

Think about some of the situations that make you feel anxious

It is pretty normal to feel anxious in certain situations, but usually the feeling of anxiety goes away when the situation is over. While anxious feelings aren't pleasant and can be a bit distressing, they can also be a positive thing because they may mean you are doing something challenging or adventurous, and afterwards you will probably have a wonderful sense of achievement and pride.

Also, being a bit anxious can actually be healthy at times because it can help us to be more alert — for example, when we are in risky situations such as crossing a busy road or learning to climb a rock wall.

However, if a person has anxious feelings most of the time (even when he or she is not in a stressful situation) and is prevented from having a normal life, it may mean that they have an anxiety disorder. If this seems to be happening to you or someone you know, it is important to talk to someone you trust, and seek advice from a health professional such as the school counsellor or your family doctor.

Bullying

Bullying is when someone gets repeatedly picked on, put down or harassed by others. It is usually done with the intention of hurting someone and making them feel scared, threatened and distressed.

What can you do if you are being bullied?
The first thing to remember is that bullying is never OK and something should always be done about it. The sooner something is done, the better. When the bullying is actually happening, it may be better to just walk away if you can. This doesn't mean you should ignore the problem. In fact, it is vital that you talk about it to someone such as your parents, carer or a teacher, depending on where the bullying is happening.

You could try to talk to the bully — it's better if you do this away from his or her friends, and you may want to have someone with you. Tell the bully in a

Did you know?

About bullying

There are lots of ways people can bully others, including:

- Calling people rude names
- Physically hurting someone
- Saying nasty things about people or spreading rumours about them
- Playing mean jokes on another person
- Hiding or damaging another person's property
- Purposely excluding someone from activities or conversations
- Using social media, email or text messages to send nasty messages or spread rumours (cyberbullying)

As you can see, bullying may not always be obvious. People may be bullied about the way they look, their ability to do things, their religion, race, sexuality, the people they hang out with or even about the clothes they wear. Bullying is treated very seriously in most places. In workplaces, bullies can get fired from their job.

very firm way that you don't like what they are doing, and that you expect it to stop. This can be difficult to do, and of course may not work, and if it doesn't you will need to talk about it with someone. Most schools have very strong rules about bullying and have a legal obligation to protect you.

It is also important to make sure you don't become a bully yourself. Just because you may not like someone, or are annoyed by them, doesn't mean you have to give them a hard time.

What can you do if you see someone else being bullied?

If you see someone else being bullied and don't do anything, the bullying will just get worse. It may be a bit scary to get involved, and you may not want to be seen as a 'tell tale', but everyone has some responsibility to stop bullying happening. It is up to all of us to make sure that people are treated with respect and feel safe.

What is cyberbullying?

Technologies such as texting, mobile phone cameras, emails, forums, apps, social networking sites and blogs can be good ways to communicate with family and friends. Unfortunately, some people (sometimes called trolls) use this technology to bully others by sending rude, hurtful or abusive messages and images, impersonating others, teasing or spreading nasty rumours or purposely excluding someone. This is called cyberbullying.

What can you do if you are being cyberbullied?

Just like other types of bullying, cyberbullying is never OK. It can feel overwhelming, but even if you are upset, embarrassed or anxious, it can be stopped.

If it is happening to you:
- Don't respond to the bullying posts, texts or emails.
- Tell an adult you trust such as a parent or school teacher.
- Collect evidence by keeping the text messages, emails or online conversations.
- Change your privacy settings and, if possible, block contact from that person on your phone or website.
- You may want to ask someone to report the abuse to the social media service.

If you know someone else who is being bullied:
- Tell an adult you trust, such as a parent or school teacher.
- Don't join in by making comments about the messages or images and don't forward them on to anyone.
- Stop participating in those conversations.
- If you feel confident enough, ask the bullies to stop.
- Support your friend by letting them know you are there for them.

It is important to respect your friends and others. Remember, always treat others as you would like to be treated.

For you to think about

Things you can do in order to be mentally healthy

- Talk about your thoughts and feelings with friends, family or a counsellor — this can help you solve your problems and feel less stressed and anxious

- Do things you enjoy and find relaxing — this may include reading, listening to music, relaxation exercises, daydreaming or being with friends

- Exercise regularly, eat nutritious food and get adequate sleep — all these can help you feel physically well, which in turn can relieve stress and anxiety

- Don't be afraid to ask for help — some problems are easier to solve with help, and it is important not to try to solve everything yourself. Another person may have a different perspective or approach, which may help

- Family or friends may be able to provide all the help you need; but some problems can be too difficult or complex and that is when professional advice from a family doctor, school counsellor or social worker is important — they are there to help

Online safety

Many young people are spending more and more time online, texting, chatting or gaming. While there are great benefits of being online, there are other risks apart from cyberbullying.

Social networking is a great way to stay in touch with friends and family but it's important to understand the risks of sharing information online. You need to protect your privacy and the privacy of your friends. Photos and videos that are OK for friends to see may not be appropriate to be shared with people they don't know. Something you might think is funny, such as a silly photo of your friends, may not seem funny to them and may be hurtful or embarrassing.

Don't post anything online about anyone that you wouldn't say to them face to face. Once something is put on the internet you don't have any control over who sees it.

It is important not to share personal information such as your account details, passwords or your address. This information may be used inappropriately by people you don't know. Remember, it is easy for people to lie online so you need to think carefully about how well you really know your online friends.

It's very easy to get carried away and spend more time than you intend to online. Long periods online mean other activities such as exercise, talking with friends and sleep can be neglected. It may also cause conflict, as your parents might be concerned about the amount of time you spend online.

To stay safe online:

- Limit your time online and make time for offline activities such as seeing friends, physical activities and other things you enjoy.
- Be careful about who you 'friend' or 'follow' online.
- Don't share personal details (including your phone number, your address or which school you attend).
- Don't give your password to anyone and make sure your profile is set to private.
- Remember: it's easy for people to lie online and people can pretend they are someone they are not. You should never arrange to meet anyone you have met online unless you have your parents' permission.
- Be careful about the photos or videos you post.
- Think carefully before you post, upload or download anything.
- Tell someone you trust if you are worried about anything that is happening online.

Chapter 6

Learning about sex

Many of the changes that happen at puberty are to do with sex and being able to have children. Often people think they are not sexual until they are actually having sexual intercourse, but being sexual means more than just having intercourse. People can feel sexual when they think about sexy things, when they kiss and cuddle someone they like, when they touch themselves in places that feel good or when they read or watch sexy or romantic stories.

The changes that happen to young people at puberty may also result in an increase in sexual feelings. Some young people may find themselves thinking about sex more often and having strong sexual feelings. Because we are all different and develop at different rates, some young people will not have sexual feelings and will not be interested in sex at all until they are much older.

What is sex all about?
— girl, 11 years

All people think and feel differently about sex.

Sex means different things to different people, and all people think and feel differently about sex. Sex or sexuality means more than having sexual intercourse. It also includes how people feel about themselves, and how they feel about their bodies. Many people do not talk about sex, and as a result they are often confused and ignorant about it.

For people to make important decisions about sex — whether or not to have it, when to have it, who to have it with, whether or not to have children — they need to have lots of information. They also need to learn how to make their own decisions and not be pressured into doing anything they don't want to do or are not sure about. Most of all, people need to feel good about themselves and their bodies.

Sexual intercourse

Sexual intercourse is when an erect penis enters a female's vagina. The couple then move in and out in a way that feels pleasurable to both. Usually the couple spend time kissing, cuddling and touching each other before they have sexual intercourse; this is called foreplay, and usually causes them to become very aroused, which makes sexual intercourse more pleasurable. Sometimes people just do these sexy things without actually having intercourse.

What is an orgasm? — *girl, 12 years*
Sometimes the very pleasant feelings people have when they are sexually aroused will result in an orgasm. An orgasm is a climax of the sexual feelings and involves a high level of sexual excitement. It includes contractions of the muscles of the pelvis and a pleasant feeling that spreads throughout the body. The male orgasm usually happens at the same time as ejaculation. Sexual intercourse isn't necessary for an orgasm; people can also have an orgasm when masturbating or having their genitals stimulated in other ways that they like.

Why do people have sex? — *girl, 11 years*
People have sexual intercourse for many different reasons. They may have sex to have babies, to show they love each other or because it is enjoyable, or for a combination of these reasons.

Do you have to have an erection to have sexual intercourse? — *boy, 12 years*
Yes, the penis needs to be firm to be able to go into the vagina, although men can still get pleasant sexual feelings without necessarily having an erection.

When to have sex

There are many different opinions about when people should first have sexual intercourse. In Ireland it is against the law for someone under 17 to have sex.

Mum and Dad think it is wrong to have sex before marriage or to get pregnant before marriage. Is it?
— *girl, 12 years*

Some people do feel very strongly about sex before marriage, believing it is morally wrong for you to have sex with anyone other than your husband or wife. Other people feel differently about this.

It is good to discuss these things with your parents or other people you feel comfortable with. As you get older and think more about sex, you will develop your own attitudes and values. These may be similar to your parents' or they may be different. It's important not to hurry into decisions on such complicated matters.

What age would you recommend to have sex?
— *boy, 13 years*

There is no particular age when you are guaranteed to be ready to have sex. It will depend on many issues, including your maturity, whether you really want to have sex, your moral and religious values and the type of relationship you are in. Many young people have mixed feelings about whether they want to have sex or not. If you are unsure or do not feel ready to have a sexual relationship, it is better for you to wait.

Did you know?

About the age of consent

In many places it is illegal for a girl or boy under the age of 17 to have sexual intercourse. The age of consent may vary a little from country to country and state to state.

Is it good to have sex when you are young?
— *boy, 12 years*

Although it is impossible to say what is the right age to have sex, most people in their early teens are not mature enough to cope with the responsibilities that go with having sex. Also, in Ireland it is against the law for someone under 17 to have sex.

If a boy asks you to have sex and you are only young, what do you say? — *girl, 13 years*

The best thing to say is 'no' in a firm voice. You don't have to give a reason unless you want to. It is best if you wait until you are older, and sure it is what you want to do and that you are ready for it, before you have sex. A sexual relationship brings with it lots of responsibility, like preventing unwanted pregnancies, avoiding sexually transmitted infections and protecting each other from being emotionally hurt or disappointed. All of these issues are easier to deal with if you are mature and generally more experienced.

How often do people have sex? — *boy, 12 years*
It is difficult to answer this, as it will vary from person to person. Some people have sex frequently, some have sex only occasionally and some people do not have sex at all. No one can say what is normal and what is not normal, as different people have different levels of desire for sex, and these levels can change throughout their lives.

The main thing to remember is that people should make their own decisions about sexual activity, and should be aware of the responsibilities that go with sexual activity. It is also important for people in a relationship to be able to talk to each other about sex, to feel comfortable telling each other what they like and don't like, and to agree on how often they would like to have sex.

Does everyone have to have sex?
— *girl, 11 years*
No, not everyone has sex, and some people make a definite decision not to become sexually active, or to cease sexual activity. Some people belonging to religious groups make a vow not to have sex, so that they can concentrate totally on their religion. Other people may just decide that sexual activity is not important to them. Not having sex, for whatever reason, is called celibacy.

Do all people like sexual intercourse?
— *girl, 12 years*

> No one can say what is normal and what is not normal.

Some people may enjoy sex very much, while others may not always, or ever, enjoy sex. This will depend on whether they want to have sex in the first place. If people are forced into having sex when they don't want to they will not enjoy it. This is why it is important for people always to make their own choice, and only to have sex when they feel ready.

Do you think sex is hyped up to be more than it is?
— *girl, 14 years*

In the last few decades, people have become much more aware of sex and issues to do with sexuality than they were in the past. People are now more willing to talk about sex, and this is generally good in that people are more ready to learn and communicate with each other about sex. However, sex is also used in advertising to sell a whole range of products that have nothing to do with sex, like cars, food and household goods. This can cause people to think that sex dominates everything they do, and as a result some people have unrealistic expectations of sex.

In reality, sex is just one aspect of a person's personality and their relationship. For some people sex is quite important, but generally a loving and supportive relationship is much more important.

Attitudes towards sex

1920's

2000's

Sssh!

Have you got a condom?

Is it true that people's attitudes towards sexual intercourse have changed? — *girl, 13 years*

Certainly in the last few decades, sexuality has come to be discussed more openly; however, many parents still find it difficult to talk to their children about sex. There are certainly some people who think it is OK to have sexual intercourse before marriage, but others think that it is not OK.

It is difficult to tell whether people are having sex earlier in life than they were, say, 50 years ago. In the past people got married much younger. However, most would agree that it is best for people to have sexual intercourse only when they are mature and ready to accept the responsibilities that go with having a sexual relationship.

How many ways are there of having sex?
— *boy, 11 years*

There are many ways of having sex. Being sexually active does not just mean having sexual intercourse. People can have strong sexual feelings during masturbation, kissing, cuddling, touching or thinking about sex. When people have sexual intercourse, they may try many different positions (for instance, one person may be on top of the other, they may be side by side or they may be lying or sitting), or they may always have sex in one position. Many people also have oral sex.

The main thing is for people to be able to communicate to each other about what they like or don't like, and to feel comfortable and secure with what they are doing.

What is oral sex? — *boy, 10 years*

This is when a person uses the mouth or tongue on the genitals of the other person to give sexual pleasure. A woman cannot get pregnant through oral sex. Sexually transmitted infections can be passed on through oral sex, especially if the person giving oral sex has mouth ulcers or gum disease.

Why is the boy always on the girl's body?
— *boy, 12 years*

The man isn't always on top — although many movies portray sex this way. In reality, people have sexual intercourse in different positions depending on how comfortable they feel and how pleasurable it is for them.

What is the best possible position for sex?
— *boy, 11 years*
It is difficult to say what is the best position, as different people have different preferences.

How long does sex take? — *boy, 11 years*
This also will vary, depending on the individual and the circumstances. Some people become sexually aroused very quickly and sex may not last very long at all, maybe only a few minutes. Other people will want to make it last longer. However, having sexual intercourse does take a bit of energy, and it is tiring. People can't keep going forever.

Is sex fun? — *boy, 12 years*
Sex can be lots of fun. Again, it depends on the circumstances. If both partners want to have sex together and are protected against unwanted pregnancy or catching an STI, it is more likely to be enjoyable.

People are not going to enjoy sex if they are unsure if they want to have sex, if they are forced into having sex or if they are worried about pregnancy or catching an STI.

Does sex hurt? — *girl, 12 years*
Sex usually does not hurt. However, it can be uncomfortable or painful, especially for women if they are not

fully aroused or not comfortable with their decision to have intercourse. If a woman is forced into having sex, it will probably be painful for her. When a man is sexually aroused his penis becomes erect, and when a woman is aroused her vagina becomes soft and moist and the penis will fit in more comfortably. If a woman does not become aroused enough she may experience discomfort and pain during intercourse. When a couple have sex for the first time, they should take it slowly and gently. It is very important for people to be ready and happy with their decision to have sex.

Sometimes, males or females experience pain during sexual intercourse as the result of some kind of infection or disease. In this case it is worth going to the doctor for a check-up.

What would happen if you have sexual intercourse during a period? — *girl, 13 years*

There is no reason why people can't have sex during a women's period, as long as the couple feel OK about it. Some people think that a woman cannot get pregnant if she has sex during her period. This is not true, so it is important to continue using contraception at this time to avoid pregnancy.

Boys get erections. Do girls get anything? — *boy, 12 years*

When a male is sexually aroused, the blood supply to the penis increases and the penis becomes hard, erect and more sensitive. When a female is sexually aroused,

> In both males and females the nipples become erect, and the heart rate and breathing quicken.

the blood supply to her genital area increases. This causes her vagina to become softer and more moist and her clitoris to become hard and more sensitive. In both males and females the nipples become erect, and the heart rate and breathing quicken.

What is sexting? – *girl, 11 years*

Sexting is when someone sends sexual messages, photos or videos, in a text or by posting online. It is usually done as a joke or as innocent flirting. However, one of the problems with sexting is that the message can be widely distributed and the person who first sent the text has no control over where it goes. These messages or photos may be embarrassing or damage a person's reputation and can lead to cyberbullying.

There are also legal consequences as it is against the law to take or distribute sexually explicit images of people under the age of 18 years. Sexting is a crime at any age if it involves harassing people.

It is best not to send or publish images of yourself or to distribute any that friends have sent to you. If you have sent something you regret to a friend, ask them to delete it immediately. If you are concerned about anything that is posted online, talk to someone you trust.

Homosexuality

A person who is *homosexual* is attracted to and may have a sexual relationship with someone of the same sex. Female homosexuals are often referred to as lesbians and male homosexuals are often referred to as gay. *Heterosexual* people are attracted to and may have a sexual relationship with someone of the other sex. A person who is *bisexual* is attracted to and may have sex with both men and women.

While most people are in heterosexual relationships, a small percentage of people are homosexual.

It is not uncommon for young people to have strong sexual feelings for someone of their own sex and some adolescents think this means they are homosexual. These feelings are a normal part of sexual development, along with lots of different kinds of other sexual feelings. Many people's first sexual thoughts or fantasies will be about people of the same sex. Perhaps this is because their stronger friendships at this time are with people of the same sex.

How come there are homosexuals and lesbians in the world? — boy, 12 years
Nobody really knows why some people have sexual relationships with people of the same sex. What we do know is that homosexual people cannot change their sexual orientation, just as heterosexuals can't change theirs. They are probably born this way, or something may have influenced them as they grew up; it may be a combination of both of these things.

How do you become gay? — *girl, 12 years*
People don't usually decide to become gay or lesbian. Most homosexual people feel that this is just the way they are, and that they don't have any choice about their sexual orientation.

How do gay and lesbian people have sex? Do they enjoy it? — *girl, 13 years*
Homosexuals express their sexuality in similar ways to heterosexuals. This may include touching, kissing, cuddling and having oral sex. Some gay men have anal sex. Anal sex is when a man puts his penis in the anus (back passage) of another person.

Homosexual people enjoy sex, just as heterosexual couples do. Most also enjoy a loving and caring relationship.

Homophobia

Homophobia is when someone has negative feelings towards or fears someone who is or may be thought to be homosexual. This can be displayed as rejection, bullying or violence. This discrimination can come from ignorance, fear and immaturity. Name-calling, bullying and violence are never OK. If you have experienced any form of homophobia or you know someone who has, tell someone you trust or talk to a counsellor.

Masturbation

Masturbation means touching or rubbing your own or another person's genital area, especially the penis or clitoris, to give sexual pleasure. It may also be pleasurable to touch other parts of the body. People may have sexual thoughts while they are masturbating. Masturbation is one way of getting sexual pleasure, with or without a sexual partner. Not all people masturbate. Some people have never done it and don't want to.

> Masturbation is a normal and healthy way of getting sexual pleasure for males and females.

I masturbate. Am I normal? — *boy, 12 years*
Yes, masturbation is a normal and healthy way of getting sexual pleasure. When young people reach puberty they often have strong sexual feelings and masturbation is a good way of releasing these feelings. If you do masturbate, it is best if you're in a private place where you won't be disturbed. It is against the law to masturbate in public.

**Is there anything wrong with masturbation at all?
— *boy, 12 years***
No, there is nothing wrong with masturbation. However, if people have strong religious or personal beliefs that masturbation is wrong it might make them feel guilty.

When sex is never OK

Sexual abuse

Sexual abuse is when an older person or adult does sexual things to a child. The older person may touch the child's breasts or genital area, or make the child touch the person's genital area. When this happens within a family it is called incest. Although a child often feels very confused and may find the situation difficult to talk about, it is important for him/her to tell someone because sexual abuse is *always* wrong.

Children may tell a parent, or may need to tell an adult outside the family who they feel they can trust. Sometimes that person finds it hard to believe that such a thing has happened; however, it is important for the child not to give up. Someone else — a brother or sister, an aunt or grandparent, a teacher or a friend's mother — may be more helpful.

Sexual abuse can also include an adult saying things to a child that make the child feel uncomfortable. Sometimes a child may not know whether the things the adult is saying or doing are actually wrong. If any adult does something to you and tells you not to tell your parents or anyone else, he/she is most likely doing something that is wrong. If you are not sure, you can ask yourself some questions to help you sort it out:

- Does this person touch me in a way that makes me feel uncomfortable?
- Does it hurt when they touch me?

- Do they touch the private parts of my body?
- Do they tell me to keep it a secret?
- Do they continue to do it even when I tell them to stop?
- Do they say they will punish me if I tell anyone?
- Do they say things to me that make me feel uncomfortable?

If anyone touches the private parts of your body or touches you in a way that hurts or makes you feel uncomfortable, say 'no' very firmly. Tell them to stop what they are doing, to go away and that you will tell someone.

You have a right to feel safe.

If you are being abused and the abuse stays a secret, the situation is unlikely to change. You will need to tell someone so that they can help you stop it happening. It is important for you to remember that you have done nothing wrong, and you have a right to feel safe.

Sometimes friends might tell you about things that are happening to them that they don't like, or they might come straight out and tell you they are being abused. If this happens, try to be understanding and listen to them, and get them to tell an adult. They could telephone the police, the appropriate government agency or a counselling service.

Remember the three steps —
NO, STOP and I'LL TELL!

Rape

Rape is when someone is forced to have sexual intercourse against his/her will. Rape is an act of violence and humiliation, and is against the law. Rape is often called sexual assault. It is mostly females who are sexually assaulted, but it can happen to males as well. Many people think rapes are attacks by strangers in dark, isolated streets. This may sometimes happen, but usually people are raped by someone they know. It may be a person they have just met or it may be someone they know well.

Most people who have been raped will need to talk to someone about it. Some people will decide to report it to the police, so that the rapist can be caught, charged and punished. However, some people decide not to do this, as they do not want to go through the process of reporting it and having to go over all the details with the police and in court. This decision is up to the individual, but for most people it will help them if they can find someone who will give lots of support and understanding to help them get over this traumatic experience.

They may be able to talk to a member of their family, or a friend, or they may like to talk to a counsellor or someone who works specifically in this area. Most cities have rape crisis centres and telephone counselling services for people who have been raped. These are easily found online.

Chapter 7

Fertilisation, pregnancy and birth

Attitudes to pregnancy and birth have changed a lot in the last 50 years. Many of your grandparents or parents would be able to recall knowing nothing about the birth of their younger brothers or sisters except that their mother's stomach grew large, she disappeared for a few days and then returned home with a baby! No one explained where it came from, or how it got in or out. Perhaps the stork brought it or it was found in the cabbage patch!

Many people were quite ignorant themselves, leaving the knowledge and the decisions about their child's birth to doctors and nurses. The baby's father usually had very little involvement, and was rarely present at the baby's birth, unlike many dads today.

Today, women are much better informed and more involved. With the availability of reliable contraceptive methods, we can usually plan the timing and the number of pregnancies. Most women can choose where they will have their babies, who will be present at the birth and to some extent the type of labour and delivery they will have.

Pregnancy and birth for many women is now a family affair, and older brothers and sisters are often encouraged to learn about the pregnancy as it progresses, feeling the baby move inside the mother and perhaps hearing its heartbeat or seeing ultrasound photos or a video taken before it is even born.

Most children will meet their little brother or sister very soon after its birth, and some may even see it born. Today the experience of childbirth isn't hidden away or treated like an illness. Instead it can be celebrated by the whole family for what it is — the making of a new life and a very wonderful event!

Fertilisation

How do you get pregnant? — *girl, 10 years*

If a girl has started having periods and has sexual intercourse, she may become pregnant unless the couple are using a reliable form of contraception. The sperm from the semen will move up through her cervix and uterus into the fallopian tubes. If the woman has ovulated (released an ovum/egg) in the previous day or two, one of the sperm may penetrate the ovum, causing fertilisation. If an ovum isn't present, a pregnancy cannot start; it takes both an ovum from the woman and a sperm from the man to start a pregnancy.

Once fertilisation has taken place, the cells start to divide and multiply. As this is happening, the fertilised ovum moves down the fallopian tube to the uterus, taking about five days. There, it attaches itself to the lining and continues to develop.

How many times do you have sex before you have a baby? — *girl, 12 years*

This will vary from couple to couple. Some women become pregnant the first time they have sexual intercourse; for others it may take a number of months of having sex regularly. A small percentage of couples will have difficulty achieving a pregnancy, and some may never have a pregnancy. Many of these couples will be able to have a baby after they have tests and treatment.

What's the right age to have a baby? — *girl, 11 years*

There is no such thing as the 'right' age to have a baby. Every woman should decide what is the right age for her. Some women decide never to have a baby. Factors that should be considered include whether a woman is financially secure, whether she has finished her education, whether she is emotionally ready to become a parent and whether she has enough financial and emotional support.

Some people believe that a woman should only have a baby after she is married. The choice will be different for every female. Whatever the reasons, for women and men, their lifestyle will certainly be different once they become parents.

Did you know?

About fertility

- A woman is most fertile when she ovulates, usually during the middle of her menstrual cycle. She can only get pregnant for a few days either side of ovulation. Sometimes it's difficult to tell exactly when this happens, as the menstrual cycle may be different from month to month.
- Some animal species can only get pregnant at a certain time of year, such as spring. That way, their young will be born when the weather and other conditions are most suitable. Humans, however, can get pregnant during any season.

Becoming pregnant

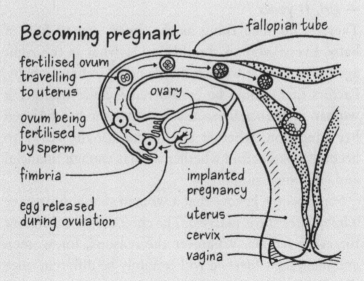

fallopian tube

fertilised ovum travelling to uterus

ovary

ovum being fertilised by sperm

fimbria

implanted pregnancy

egg released during ovulation

uterus

cervix

vagina

Why can't some people have babies?
— *girl, 10 years*

Some people choose not to have children. However, some people, although they may desperately want to have children, may be unable to. There are many different causes of infertility, and the cause may lie with the woman, the man or with both. The woman may not ovulate, or she may have a blockage in one of her fallopian tubes. Infertility in the male can be caused by an absence or low number of sperm, or sperm that do not move properly. In some cases the cause of infertility is unknown. However, knowledge of infertility and ways to overcome it are increasing all the time.

What's a test-tube baby? — *boy, 11 years*

The correct name for 'test-tube baby' is 'in vitro fertilisation', which is from the Latin word meaning 'in glass'. It refers to the fertilisation of an ovum or egg by a sperm outside the woman's uterus, in a container called a petri dish (not a test tube). In vitro fertilisation may be used if a woman or man is infertile. The first in vitro fertilisation baby was born in Britain in 1978.

How do you get twins? — *girl, 9 years*

Most women only have one baby at a time, but about one pregnancy in 90 is a twin pregnancy. There are two types of twins, fraternal (dizygotic) twins and identical (monozygotic) twins.

Did you know?

About animal babies

- The armadillo always has four babies, identical quadruplets.
- Kangaroos may have one baby just out of the pouch and still at foot, one in its pouch and one growing in its uterus.
- The female pig has a pregnancy of 115 days (16 weeks) and may carry more than twelve babies at the one time.
- A Great Dane is recorded as having had a litter of 23 puppies — 16 of them survived.

With fraternal twins two ova are released by the woman and these are fertilised by two different sperm. These twins are not identical and may be two boys, two girls or one of each. Identical twins happen when one ovum is fertilised by one sperm and in the early stages of cell division the fertilised ovum divides completely in two, allowing for two individuals to develop. Identical twins are always the same sex.

Could you have three babies at a time?
— boy, 9 years
Yes, it is possible, but the chance of a woman having three babies (triplets) at the same time is about one in 8100.

Did you know?

About Siamese twins

The name Siamese twins comes from the famous conjoined twins Chang and Eng Bunker who were born in Siam (now Thailand) in 1811. Chang and Eng were joined at the chest and died within a few hours of each other at the age of 62. They married sisters and between them fathered 22 children. Conjoined twins are very rare and it is probably because of this that we hear so much about them when they are born. Some conjoined twins can be surgically separated, depending on where they are joined.

How are Siamese twins made? — *boy, 11 years*
The correct name is conjoined twins. Conjoined twins are identical twins that did not divide completely in half in the very early stages of the pregnancy so that they remain joined together.

Can women still have babies over 50 years of age? — *girl, 12 years*
Yes, it is possible, but very rare. Most women go through menopause between the ages of 45 and 55. This means that they stop having periods and producing ova. Once this happens, a woman can't get pregnant.

However, there are some exceptions. It is thought that the oldest woman to give birth was 63 years old when she gave birth in California, USA. Recently, advances in medical technology have made it possible for women past menopause to become pregnant, but it is unlikely that this technology will become available to all women.

Is it true that if you get punched hard in the stomach it will make you not be able to have children? — *girl, 13 years*

Being punched hard in the stomach won't make a woman infertile. Nor would a kick in the testicles make a man infertile. Only a very severe accident would cause fertile men and women to become infertile.

How can a woman tell if she's pregnant? — *girl, 14 years*

The first physical sign that a woman is pregnant is that her periods stop, although many women suspect that they might be pregnant before they miss their first period. The most common way to confirm pregnancy is with a urine test a week or so after the period was due. This test is available from doctors and family planning centres or by using a home pregnancy test purchased at the chemist.

If a woman is very eager to know if she is pregnant, she can have a blood test that will indicate her pregnancy a little earlier.

Pregnancy

Do you still get your periods when you are pregnant? — *girl, 13 years*

No, a woman's periods will stop while she is pregnant. If she experiences any bleeding once her pregnancy is confirmed, she should see her doctor.

> A woman's periods will stop while she is pregnant.

When pregnant, should people stop having sex?
— *boy, 13 years*

As long as the pregnancy is progressing normally, there is no reason why a couple cannot continue to have sex right up until the baby is born, as long as they both want to and it is comfortable for them.

How long is the baby in the woman's womb?
— *girl, 11 years*

On average, a pregnancy will last for nine months (40 weeks).

Do all babies stay in the womb for nine months?
— *girl, 11 years*

No, sometimes a baby is born earlier or a little bit later, although rarely more than 42 weeks. If a baby is born before 37 weeks it is said to be premature or pre-term.

Did you know?

About the length of pregnancies

In the animal world pregnancy lengths vary and range from a couple of weeks in some smaller marsupials, such as mice or opossums, to nearly two years for the Asian elephant. The cow and the gorilla both have similar lengths of pregnancy to humans.

Stages of pregnancy

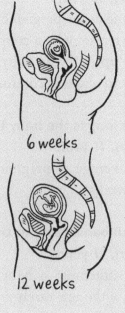

6 weeks
The embryo is less than 1.5 cm long - about the size and shape of a jellybean. The buds where the arms and legs will grow are just visible.

6 weeks

12 weeks
The foetus is about 9 cm long and weighs about 140 grams. Its shape is now recognisably human.

12 weeks

20 weeks (halfway)
Most pregnant women
can feel the baby
moving by this stage.
It is about 25 cm long
and weighs about
300 grams.

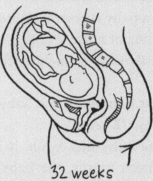

20 weeks

32 weeks
With expert care a
baby born at this
stage would have a
chance of surviving.
Its length is about
43 cm and weighs
about 1800 grams.

32 weeks

40 weeks (Full term)
An average full term
baby weighs about
3500 grams and will
be about 50 cm long,
but this will vary a
great deal.

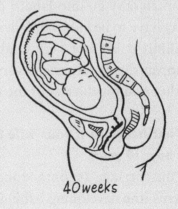

40 weeks

How do you get premature babies?
— *girl, 12 years*

Pre-term babies are not uncommon, and for many of them there is no apparent reason why the labour began early. It may be because there are abnormalities with the uterus or the cervix, or it may be that the mother has an illness such as high blood pressure. Sometimes, because of problems with the pregnancy, the labour may be induced, or started early, with the use of drugs.

If a baby is born early it may have to be cared for in a neonatal nursery until it can breathe on its own and suck strongly enough to feed.

What happens if the baby dies in the womb?
— *boy, 12 years*

If the baby dies while it is still growing inside the mother's uterus, the baby has to be delivered. The woman may go into labour on her own or the labour may have to be induced. A dead baby is called stillborn. Stillbirths are not very common, but when they do happen the experience is very sad for the mother, the father and for the rest of the family.

What happens if your wife has a miscarriage?
— *boy, 10 years*

A miscarriage (spontaneous abortion) is when the foetus (the developing baby) is delivered before twenty weeks of pregnancy. About 15 per cent of pregnancies end in miscarriage and in the majority of these it is believed that the foetus was not developing properly. When a woman has a miscarriage she is likely to be very upset. If she has someone to talk to and support her it will help her to grieve and recover.

How does a woman get a sick baby if she smokes?
— *girl, 11 years*

If a woman smokes when she is pregnant, the blood flow to the placenta is reduced. This means that the oxygen supply and nourishment of the developing baby will be restricted, resulting in low birth weight. Smoking during pregnancy also increases the risk of stillbirth and premature birth.

What causes a baby to become deformed?
— *boy, 10 years*

Sometimes it is not known why a baby is born with an abnormality. It may be due to abnormal chromosomes, an inherited syndrome or exposure to chemicals, drugs or radiation, especially during early pregnancy.

Is there more chance of an older woman's baby having faults? — *girl, 9 years*

Today many women are in their late thirties or early forties when they have their first baby, having established careers or become financially secure first or perhaps just feeling ready by that age. Women who have their first pregnancy when they are over 35 may be at higher risk of developing complications during their pregnancy.

However, good general health at the beginning of the pregnancy is very important. The risk of some genetic abnormalities, such as Down's Syndrome, does increase with age — and the age of the father may be just as much a factor as the age of the mother. If both parents are in good health, and the mother has regular check-ups during the pregnancy, she is likely to have a healthy pregnancy and a healthy baby.

Can anything happen to the baby if the woman falls on her stomach? — *boy, 10 years*

It is very unlikely that the developing baby will be damaged if the woman falls when she is pregnant. The accident would have to be extremely serious for the baby to be hurt. The mother's body, and the fluid that surrounds the baby during the pregnancy, provide excellent protection for the baby from any falls or knocks.

How come men can't have babies?
— boy, 12 years

Men can't have babies because they don't have a uterus or the other reproductive organs necessary for pregnancy. They do provide the necessary sperm, however, and although the baby does not develop inside them they are responsible for 50 per cent of its genetic make-up. So the baby has just as much chance of looking like the dad as it does the mum. Even though a man can't give birth, he can still play a very active part in caring for the baby. The role of the father can be just as important as the mother.

Birth

Where does the baby come through?
— girl, 9 years
A baby can be born in two ways, either through the woman's vagina, which is the most common way for a baby to be delivered, or by Caesarean section through the abdomen wall.

How come the hole is so small? — boy, 11 years
The vagina does not need to be large because it has the ability to stretch enough for the baby to fit through and then shrink back again, a little like a thick elastic band. The same goes for the cervix, which must remain tightly closed against the weight and movement of the baby in the uterus.

What does Caesarean mean? — girl, 11 years
A Caesarean is the delivery of a baby through an incision or cut, made through the woman's abdomen and uterus. The mother is given an anaesthetic. This can be a general anaesthetic or an epidural, which numbs her below the waist but allows her to be conscious to see the baby once it is born. The wound is stitched up immediately after delivery. Caesareans are a fairly common procedure, although they are only performed if there are complications with the pregnancy or the delivery.

Caesareans are a fairly common procedure.

What are the risks with Caesareans?
— *boy, 12 years*

The risks of complications, infections or death associated with having a Caesarean is very low. At the beginning of the last century Caesareans were only given in extreme emergencies and the risks, particularly to the mother, were very high. Today, with modern techniques and the availability of antibiotics and blood transfusions, the risks are very low.

If a women is experiencing complications of pregnancy or birth, a Caesarean section is certainly safer for her and her baby than a vaginal birth. It can even save her or her baby's life.

For a woman who has a Caesarean, recovery may be slower than after a vaginal delivery and she may have to stay in hospital a few more days.

Could the baby get stuck inside you?
— *girl, 11 years*

No, not really. Some deliveries may be more difficult, and if the mother or baby are in any danger the doctor or midwife may use instruments called forceps which fit around the baby's head inside the vagina, to gently pull the baby out. If this is not possible, a Caesarean may be performed.

How are quins born? — *boy, 12 years*

The delivery of quins, or five babies, is similar to any other delivery. All multiple pregnancies (more than one baby) have a higher risk of premature births. That means the babies are born before full term (40 weeks).

Did you know?

Where the name (Caesarean) comes from?

Many people believe that the word Caesarean came into being because Julius Caesar was delivered this way. Caesareans were performed in Caesar's day, but only to deliver unborn babies whose mothers had died during childbirth. We know that Caesar's mother lived to have two more children after him, so it seems unlikely that he was born this way.

In ancient times the law that governed the delivery of babies by Caesarean was known as 'Lex Regia'. This later became 'Lex Caesaria', and it is likely that this is where the name came from. Another theory is that it comes from the Latin word 'caedere', meaning to cut.

Premature babies are usually smaller than full-term babies, and their lungs are often not fully developed, so that they may have breathing difficulties.

Because the babies are small, the mother may have quite a straightforward delivery, with each baby being delivered one at a time, usually with a gap of ten minutes or so between each delivery. Medical staff will take special care of the babies as they are born and may sometimes use instruments called forceps to protect and help deliver the babies heads. Occasionally a Caesarean will be performed just to make sure there are no difficulties with the delivery.

Did you know?

About childbirth

Some women have extra energy just before the birth of their baby. This is appropriately referred to as 'nesting', as the woman busies herself preparing her 'nest' or home for her new baby.

In the weeks leading up to labour many women experience mild contractions. Occasionally, these are mistaken for labour itself and the woman may go to the hospital or birth centre, only to be told to return home and wait a little longer.

A woman knows she is in labour when one or all of the following things occur:

- regular, painful contractions
- a 'show' — a small amount of bloodstained mucus from her vagina (this is a plug of thick mucus from the opening of the uterus coming away)
- her 'waters breaking' — the amniotic sac or bag ruptures and the liquid that has surrounded the baby throughout pregnancy begins to come out through the vagina, in a sudden gush or a gradual trickle

Labour usually lasts for a number of hours, so the woman usually has plenty of time to get to the hospital, or the place where she has arranged to have her baby. Now and then you hear stories of women who have an extremely short labour and deliver their baby at home or in the car, ambulance or taxi on the way to hospital. This doesn't happen very often.

Labour can be divided into three stages. In the first stage, the contractions cause the cervix to open up or dilate. This is usually the longest stage, and during the early part of this stage most women can go for a walk, talk with their partner, a friend or medical staff, or watch TV in between contractions. Towards the end of this stage the contractions become more frequent and stronger.

In the second stage the baby is delivered. The mother pushes down hard with each contraction, and the baby, usually head down, passes through the cervix and out through the vagina.

In the third stage the placenta is delivered. Mother and baby can then relax together and get to know each other. Often the baby is put straight to the mother's breast or cuddled very close. It is a very special time that most parents look back on with great happiness and sometimes even a tear in their eye!

Why is a baby's head sometimes purple when it's born? — boy, 11 years

Inside the womb, a baby's skin is a pale pink. At birth, most babies turn pinkish blue or purple from a temporary lack of oxygen. This does them no harm, and they generally begin to go pink again as they begin to breathe.

At birth, most babies turn pinkish blue or purple from a temporary lack of oxygen.

What's the white stuff on the baby when it is born? — girl, 10 years

This is called vernix. Vernix is a creamy substance that protects the baby's skin during the nine months it is in the uterus. It's a little like barrier cream. Some babies are born with only a little vernix in their skin creases; others have quite a lot of it on their bodies. It will rub or be washed off during the first few days of life.

After the baby is born, what happens to the cord and the womb? — girl, 11 years

After the baby is born the umbilical cord is cut and the placenta delivered. The placenta is the organ that has provided nourishment and oxygen to the baby during pregnancy, and the umbilical cord connects the baby to the placenta.

The cord and the placenta are checked by the midwife or medical staff to make sure that they are normal, and then they are disposed of, usually in an incinerator. The uterus will shrink back to its original size over the next six weeks or so.

What causes a woman to have pain during birth? — *girl, 12 years*

Pain during labour is caused by the contractions of the muscles of the uterus and sometimes the position of the baby. The contractions are powerful because they must open the cervix (neck of the uterus) and push the baby out through the vagina.

Does it hurt to have a baby? — *girl, 10 years*

Labour is painful, but how this pain is experienced varies from woman to woman. Some women do not require any pain relief at all, and manage with the support of their partner or a friend, and perhaps the use of relaxation techniques they have learnt in childbirth classes.

These days, women in childbirth are not routinely given pain relief, and can choose to have as little or as much pain relief as they need.

Other types of pain relief include a gas which the woman breathes in, painkillers such as pethidine or an epidural injection into the lower spine, which removes all sensation from the waist down. Labour can be painful, but there are other sensations involved that can make it an incredibly rewarding experience. When you hold your own child in your arms for the first time, you see the point of all your hard work.

Why do some people have their babies at home?
— *girl, 13 years*

In most countries today the majority of babies are born in hospital, but some women choose to have their babies at home in familiar, non-medical surroundings. Most of these women want the birth of their baby to be as natural as possible, with little or no medical intervention.

Today most modern maternity hospitals are providing more informal labour wards with comfortable chairs or beanbags and a TV where the woman can relax while she waits for the baby to be born.

What is the most number of babies ever born to one woman? — *boy, 9 years*

The highest number of babies born to one woman at the same time was nine to an Australian woman at the Royal Women's Hospital in Sydney in 1971. None of the babies lived for more than a few days.

How long does it take for the baby to leave the hospital? — *girl, 12 years*

Most women will remain in hospital with their baby for two to five days after the birth. Some will

Did you know?

About the birth of other animals

- The Australian platypus and echidna lay eggs, but after hatching the babies feed on milk, which is secreted onto the skin surface rather than being sucked from a nipple.
- Guinea pigs are born very mature and only need milk for a few days.
- The young of cattle, sheep, horses and pigs are relatively advanced at birth and can run, jump and follow their mother within a few hours of being born. They all need milk for several weeks.

choose to go home earlier, and as long as there are no complications, there is no reason why they shouldn't.

If a woman has had a Caesarean or a difficult labour, or if the baby is small or requires medical attention, they may remain in hospital for a longer period. Sometimes the mother may go home before the baby; this is quite common if the baby is born premature.

How does the milk get into the breasts?
— *girl, 11 years*
After a baby is born a hormone called prolactin is released by the mother's pituitary gland and stimulates the production of milk. The milk is produced in cells in the breast. The ingredients needed to make the milk

come from the mother's blood. Once breastfeeding is established, the regular sucking of the nipple by the baby causes more prolactin to be released. This maintains the milk supply for the baby.

Breastmilk is the ideal food for babies, and all women should be encouraged to breastfeed if they can. For a number of reasons some women may not be able to, or may not wish to breastfeed their babies. These babies will be fed with infant formula from a bottle. Whether a baby is breast or bottlefed, it will usually thrive, particularly if it receives lots of love, affection and care.

For you to discuss with a parent or an adult who cares about you

- What was your birth like? Who was present at the birth? What were your mother's first words when you were born?
- What did you look like? Did you have any hair? How big were you?
- Have a look through family photo albums together.
- What age do you think is a good age to have a baby?
- How would you decide when the right time was for you? What sort of things should be considered?
- When you grow up do you think you would like to have children? How many?

Chapter 8

As you get older

As you get older there are a number of ways to keep yourself sexually healthy. This includes having regular medical check-ups. It also includes practising safe sex to avoid sexually transmitted infections and prevent an unplanned pregnancy. Now, you are probably saying to yourself, 'But if I'm not having sex, why should I know about all of this?' This is all information to learn gradually and then store away for later when it is relevant. No one learns everything about a subject in one sitting. For example, we start learning about road safety when we are little children, holding a parent's hand as we cross the road. Gradually we learn about traffic lights, the dangers of speeding or drink driving, all well before we are ready to get a driver's licence.

If you learn about keeping sexually healthy now, when you are older and ready to have a sexual relationship you will have had time to think about what you've learnt, ask questions about anything

you're unclear about, discuss it all thoroughly and form your own attitudes.

Contraception

Contraception can be used when people have sexual intercourse but want to avoid a pregnancy. In the past, women may have had many pregnancies, sometimes 15 or 20, because a reliable method of contraception was not available. Today, couples can choose when and how many pregnancies they have. Some people may choose not to have any children at all.

Making decisions about using contraception, and choosing what method to use, should be the responsibility of both partners. That is why it is important for people to have information about

Did you know?

About methods of contraception

- Contraceptive pill
- Emergency contraception (the 'morning-after pill')
- Condoms
- Contraceptive implant
- Contraceptive injection
- Vaginal ring
- Diaphragm
- Intrauterine device (IUD)
- Fertility awareness-based methods
- Female and male sterilisation

People who have had all the children they want or who have decided they do not want to have any children may choose sterilisation.

contraception, and to be able to communicate with each before they have sex.

Different people will have different attitudes to contraception. Some people may not use contraception for religious or cultural reasons. However, most people want to limit the number of children they have and want to plan when they have their children.

If you are sexually active, what is the best form of contraception? — *girl, 12 years*

It is difficult to say which is the best method. Some methods suit some people better than others. For protection against sexually transmitted infections, condoms are the only effective method. The contraceptive pill is one of the safest methods to prevent pregnancy, but some women are unable to take the Pill for health reasons, or do not wish to. It is good if a person or couple read all they can and discuss all the methods with a doctor or nurse and then decide which is the best method for them.

Is there any other form of contraception for women other than the Pill? — *girl, 13 years*

Yes, there are other forms of contraception a woman can use. Some women cannot use the Pill for medical reasons, so it is important for a woman to consider all the different methods and then decide which method suits her best.

What do you have to do if you don't want any more babies? — *girl, 11 years*

If a couple decide they do not want to have any more babies, they will need to use contraception every time they have sex until the woman reaches menopause, when women stop having periods and are no longer fertile. It usually happens around the age of 50. Men continue to be fertile for much longer.

If people are absolutely certain they do not want any more children, they may decide to have a sterilisation operation. The male operation is called a vasectomy; the female operation is called a tubal sterilisation.

When is the safest time to have sex?
— *girl, 13 years*
Although there are certain times in a woman's menstrual cycle when she is fertile, it is difficult to know exactly when this is. To avoid pregnancy, couples should always use a reliable method of contraception.

Fertility awareness-based methods

Fertility awareness-based methods include any method that identifies the fertile days of the menstrual cycle, when a woman is ovulating, and recommends that sexual intercourse should be avoided on these days to prevent pregnancy. Most women do this by monitoring their body, including taking their temperature and/or checking their cervical mucus, as this changes at ovulation.

Some women may find this difficult because their periods are not always regular and they have to keep detailed records. However, for some people who for religious or other reasons cannot use other methods, this may be suitable.

Emergency contraception

Emergency contraception is a method that can be used if a couple have had sex and have not used any contraception, if a condom has broken during sex or if a female has been forced to have sex and contraception was not used. Emergency contraception consists of hormonal pills. These need to be taken by the female within three days of having sex, however it is more effective if taken within 24 hours of sex. Emergency contraception is available from pharmacists, doctors and family planning clinics. This is not an ongoing method and the couple will need to use another method next time they have sex. Emergency contraception does not protect against STIs.

Condoms

A condom is made of very thin rubber and fits over the man's erect penis. If used during sexual intercourse it prevents the semen (containing sperm) going into the female vagina, and thus prevents pregnancy occurring. It also helps prevent STIs from being passed from one person to the other during sexual intercourse. Female condoms are also available.

Where can people buy condoms?
— boy, 11 years
Male condoms are sold in chemists, supermarkets, most service stations, at family planning centres and

vending machines in some public toilets and in the toilets at places such as nightclubs, hotels and airports. Female condoms are currently only available in family planning and sexual health centres and some chemists.

If you wear a condom does it feel different?
— *boy, 11 years*
Some men say that sex feels different (not as good as unprotected sex) when they use a condom. Others say it makes no difference at all. However, as condoms are a very safe method of contraception and the only method that protects against STIs, it is important for people to use them. Using a water-based lubricant with the condom may help to make sex more pleasurable.

Can a condom split during sex?
— *boy, 12 years*
Yes, condoms can break during sex, especially if they are not used properly. If they are used properly this rarely happens. If it does happen and the couple is

Did you know?

About condoms

Condoms are one of the oldest forms of contraception. Before latex rubber was invented they were usually made out of animal intestines.

worried about pregnancy, the woman can use emergency contraception.

What is a female condom? — *girl, 14 years*

The female condom is made from a type of plastic and looks similar to the male condom with a flexible ring on the either end. The woman inserts one end into her vagina while the other end sits over her vulva. It works the same way as the male condom, acting as a barrier preventing the sperm making contact with the ovum. It also helps prevent STIs, just as male condoms do.

Is there a pill to stop people having babies? — *boy, 11 years*

Yes, the contraceptive pill, if taken correctly, will prevent a pregnancy occurring. The Pill mainly works by stopping the ovaries producing ova.

Contraceptive pill

The contraceptive pill is used by many women and works by preventing the ovum maturing and being released by the ovaries. The Pill contains female hormones, the same as the hormones women already have in their bodies, but are made in a laboratory.

Women have to take the contraceptive pill at about the same time every day. It is important not to forget to take it. When a woman is on the Pill her periods are usually very regular and shorter. Some women or girls who have difficult and heavy periods may go on the Pill even if they are not having sex. If a woman wants to go on the contraceptive pill, she will need to go to a doctor or family planning centre, as it is only available on prescription. Some women may experience side effects.

Diaphragm

A diaphragm is a soft silicone device in the shape of a dome that a woman places into her vagina so that it fits over the cervix (the neck of the uterus), forming a barrier that prevents sperm entering the uterus and fertilising the ovum. It is inserted before sexual intercourse and left in for at least six hours after sex. It is important to thoroughly clean the diaphragm between uses to prevent getting an infection.

Vaginal ring

The vaginal ring is a soft plastic ring that is inserted into the vagina and remains there for three weeks and then is replaced with another one a week later. It slowly releases hormones similar to those used in the contraceptive pill.

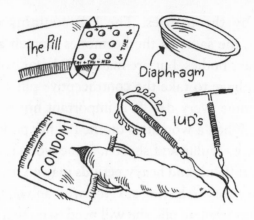

IUD

What's an IUD? — *girl, 14 years*

An IUD or intrauterine device is a small plastic device that is inserted into a women's uterus.

There are two types available: a copper IUD and a hormonal IUD. IUDs work by stopping the sperm from reaching the ovum through the fallopian tubes and preventing a fertilised ovum from attaching to the wall of the uterus. The hormonal IUD also works by preventing ovulation.

The IUD is inserted by a doctor and can stay in place for a few years. If a women wants to have a baby or decides to use another method of contraception, she can have it removed.

Contraceptive implant

The contraceptive implant is a small flexible rod which is inserted under the skin of the woman's upper arm.

Once it is inserted it slowly releases a female hormone into the blood stream to prevent pregnancy. This hormone is the same as the hormones that women already have in their bodies. The implant continues to prevent pregnancy for three years. A doctor puts in the implant.

Female and male sterilisation

Female sterilisation involves an operation or procedure that blocks the fallopian tubes. This stops the sperm joining with the ovum.

A male sterilisation operation is called a vasectomy. The vas deferens (the tube that carries the sperm to join the seminal fluid) is cut. The man still ejaculates semen during sex, but there is no sperm in it.

Before they have these operations, people must be sure that they do not want to have any more children (or any children) because the procedures are often irreversible.

Can you have your fallopian tubes tied when you are 11, 12, 13 or 14? — *girl, 12 years*
It would be very unusual for a girl of this age to have her tubes tied, as it is generally considered to be a permanent method of contraception and is only performed when a women has made the decision not to have a pregnancy. At this age a person would not be able to make a decision about sterilisation.

Can you have a certain operation that stops your periods? My mum has had a hysterectomy, I think it's called. She doesn't have her periods.
— *girl, 12 years*

In this operation the woman's uterus (womb) is removed. She no longer has periods and is not able to have any children; however, a hysterectomy is not done for these reasons, but usually because a woman has a disease of the uterus.

Abortion

A spontaneous abortion can occur when something goes wrong with a pregnancy and the embryo comes away from the uterus. This is also called a miscarriage, and usually happens very early in a pregnancy. The cause of spontaneous abortions is not always known. It may happen because there is something wrong with the developing embryo.

An induced abortion or termination of pregnancy is when the embryo and the lining of the uterus is removed using a medical procedure. It is done by a doctor, usually in a clinic or hospital. The procedure usually takes about 10 minutes and the female can go home a few hours after.

A termination of pregnancy is usually performed in the first two to three months of pregnancy.

Abortion can be an emotional topic. Some people believe it is morally wrong. However, most people believe that women should have the right to choose freely whether to have an abortion or not.

Is abortion illegal? — *girl, 12 years*

The laws regarding abortion vary from country to country. Although the laws may not always seem clear, in most countries a woman can usually have an abortion if that is what she decides she wants to do. It may be more difficult for women who live outside major cities.

If a girl thinks she is too young to have a baby, would she have an abortion? — *girl, 10 years*

This may be one reason why a girl might decide to have an abortion. There are many other reasons why abortion might be the chosen option. A female may not have planned to get pregnant and may feel that she cannot look after a baby, or she may not be well enough to have a baby. She may feel she already has enough children and cannot afford to look after any more children, or perhaps it is just not the right time. Sometimes there are a number of reasons why a woman has an abortion.

What can a woman do if she is pregnant and doesn't want to be? — *boy, 12 years*

It is good if a woman can talk to someone she feels comfortable with and think about the choices she has. She needs to make any decision regarding the pregnancy herself, and feel OK about it. She can either

For you to think about

Imagine what it was like before reliable contraception was available. Some women delivered a baby every year until menopause. Large numbers of women and babies died in childbirth because of poor health or the lack of adequate health care. The absence of reliable contraception limited their choices because they had no alternative but to bear and, unless they were very wealthy, care for children.

Could you imagine having 12 children or more in your family?

continue with the pregnancy and keep the baby, have the baby adopted or fostered out or have an abortion.

Some women who aren't at first happy about being pregnant change their minds as the pregnancy advances. It is important that, whatever a woman chooses, she makes her own decision and is not pressured by other people. There are special counselling services available in some places for women who are pregnant and need information and support.

Preventing disease
What's a Pap smear? — *girl, 12 years*
A Pap (cervical) smear is a test to locate any abnormal cells in the cervix (the neck of the uterus). It is quite a straightforward test: a doctor or nurse takes a

sample of cells from the surface of the cervix using a small spatula or brush. These cells are examined in a laboratory. Regular tests (every two years) will detect early changes well before cancer has developed. Treatment at this stage is very successful.

Do you have to have a Pap smear test if you haven't had sexual intercourse? — *girl, 13 years*

All women should have a Pap (cervical) smear within one to two years of starting to have sex, and then at least every two years until they are about 70, as long as previous tests have been normal. Even if a female has had the immunisation to protect her against infections that may cause cervical cancer, she will still need to have regular Pap smears once she starts having sex. Women who have never had sex hardly ever get cancer of the cervix, so it is probably unnecessary for them to have regular Pap (cervical) smears. If any woman is unsure about whether she should have a Pap (cervical) smear, she should check with her doctor.

Do men have Pap smear tests? — *boy, 11 years*

Men don't have a cervix, so they don't require Pap (cervical) smears; however, young men should also be aware of the benefit of keeping healthy. While cancer of the testicles is not a common disease, it is one that all men should be aware of it. From puberty onwards, men should examine their testicles regularly. If they detect a lump, a change in the shape of a testicle or any unusual swelling or pain, they should see a doctor.

Why do women have to check their breasts?
— *girl, 12 years*

All women should examine their breasts monthly for changes such as dimples, swellings or lumps. If a change is noticed she should check with her doctor. Most lumps are not cancerous.

Sexually Transmitted Infections (STIs), including HIV/AIDS

What does STI mean? — *boy, 11 years*

STI stands for sexually transmitted infection, that is, an infection passed from one person to another during sexual contact. Most STIs can be easily treated if detected.

What are the most common STIs today?
— *girl, 13 years*

The most common STIs are chlamydia, gonorrhoea, HPV, genital warts and genital herpes. Since the introduction of the vaccination against HPV, there has been a reduction in the incidence of genital warts in young people.

Ways to prevent STIs

- Don't have sex. Many people enjoy other activities that give sexual feelings, but do not run the risk of passing on or catching an STI. This might include kissing and cuddling, touching the other person's genitals or masturbating.
- Have sex with only one partner, who doesn't have sex with anyone else. This is called monogamy.
- Have tests or check-ups. If either partner has had sex, a test will diagnose any STI and this can then be treated. It may take a number of months before HIV/AIDS antibodies can be detected, so a follow-up test may be advised if risks have been taken.
- Discuss any past sexual behaviour honestly with partners.
- Always use condoms.

Can you get an STI other than from sexual intercourse? — *girl, 12 years*

Different STIs are passed on in different ways, but all can be passed on by having sexual intercourse with an infected person (unless a condom is used). Close

Did you know?

About Sexually Transmitted Infections

STIs include chlamydia, gonorrhoea, genital warts, herpes, hepatitis B, syphilis, pubic lice and HIV/AIDS.

STI symptoms might include:

- an abnormal discharge from the penis or vagina
- pain or stinging when urinating
- lumps, warts, blisters or sores around the genitals
- itchiness around the genitals
- fever
- swollen glands
- unexplained weight loss or tiredness

If you have any of these symptoms you should see a doctor for a check-up. It may not be an STI, but a doctor should be able to diagnose the cause and treat it if necessary.

Chlamydia and gonorrhoea may not cause any symptoms in women, but if they are left untreated may cause infertility — the woman may not be able to have a baby if she chooses to.

Most STIs are easily cured. Treatment might include antibiotics or a cream. STIs that cannot be cured are those caused by a virus. These include HIV/AIDS, hepatitis, genital herpes and genital warts.

sexual contact such as rubbing genitals together may also pass on an STI. HIV and hepatitis can also be passed on when the blood, semen or vaginal fluid from an infected person enters the bloodstream of another person. People who share needles when using drugs are at risk. HIV can also be passed from an infected woman to her baby during pregnancy, and possibly when breastfeeding.

What's AIDS? — *girl, 10 years*
AIDS stands for Acquired Immune Deficiency Syndrome. It is the later stage in an illness caused by a virus called Human Immunodeficiency Virus (HIV). HIV damages the human immune system so that it cannot fight off infection. People can be infected with HIV for many years before they develop AIDS. Even if they have no symptoms, the virus can still be passed on to another person.

Can AIDS kill you or only make you sick?
— *boy, 12 years*
People who are HIV positive have the virus that may lead to AIDS. They may be very healthy for many years, but most people who are HIV positive will eventually develop AIDS. People can die from AIDS; however, with treatment and a healthy lifestyle people can live a very long life.

People can be infected with HIV for many years before they develop AIDS.

Is there a way to cure AIDS? — *boy, 11 years*

At present there is no cure for HIV/AIDS; however, an HIV-infected person can take a range of medication to lengthen the time before infections occur. A healthy lifestyle will also help. Once a person has full-blown AIDS, infections may be treated with medication.

Can you get HIV from a mozzie bite?
— *girl, 11 years*

A person cannot catch HIV from a mosquito bite, from kissing, sharing cups or drinking straws or from swimming pools. The virus is not passed on during ordinary day-to-day contact.

> A person cannot catch HIV from a mosquito bite.

If the person you have had intercourse with has HIV/AIDS, do you immediately get the disease?
— *boy, 12 years*

HIV/AIDS is not always passed on during every sexual contact. However, there is no way of knowing whether it will be passed on *this time* or not, so it isn't worth taking risks. If the virus is caught, the symptoms may not show up for many years.

What is the purpose of a condom?
— *girl, 11 years*

A condom prevents semen entering another person's body during sexual intercourse; the semen remains in the condom, which is then discarded. Semen may spread HIV/AIDS if the man is infected. The man who is wearing the condom is also protected from catching an STI from his partner and his partner is protected from catching an STI from him. Condoms can also be used as a method of contraception.

Should you always use a condom when you are having sexual intercourse? — *girl, 14 years*
A couple should always use condoms when they are having sex unless they are sure that they only have sex with each other, and that neither of them had an STI when they first started having sexual intercourse. Sometimes it is difficult to be really sure. People can be tested for STIs by their doctor, at a family planning centre or at a sexual health clinic.

For you to discuss with a parent or an adult who cares about you

Did they know about STIs when they were growing up?

Do they know about and practise breast self-examination or testicular examination?

Do they have regular Pap (cervical) smear tests?

Chapter 9

Where to go for help

Even if you read this book from cover to cover, you may still have many questions left unanswered. There may be some things about which you would like even more information, now or as you get older. It is important to think about where you could get this information.

Parents

Ideally your parents would be the best place to start, but you should remember that sometimes even grown-ups can be shy or embarrassed. This may be because no one ever spoke to them about sexuality. This doesn't mean they don't want to speak to you or help you out; they just may not know how or where to start. Sometimes children need to be patient with parents, and give them time to think about the best answers or to learn about sexuality as well.

If Mum or Dad have never discussed the changes that happen as you grow up, perhaps they may need a little prompting. You could start by showing them a section of this book and telling them you would like to find out a little more or to know what they think. Reassure them that you don't expect them to know absolutely everything, but that you would enjoy hearing about their experiences and finding out more together. Remember, all of the changes that you will experience have happened to your mum or dad.

Other ways of bringing up the subject could include asking questions that are fairly easy to answer to begin with, or bringing up the experiences of friends or relatives. For example, you could tell them about a friend who had her period at school or had just bought her first bra, or about someone who has a first boyfriend or girlfriend, or discuss a friend or relative who has had a baby recently. Just let them talk about the situation for a while, and then ask about what is concerning you. If you are really shy about approaching your parents, you could try writing them a letter.

Whatever method you choose, find a moment when your parents are likely to have time, not when they have just arrived home from work or are rushing around preparing dinner. You could suggest to them that you would like to have a private chat when they have the time, without your brothers or sisters around.

Of course, you may prefer to speak with only one of your parents, but don't assume that girls must speak just with Mum and boys with Dad. Parents of the other sex can be very understanding as well.

If you don't have parents to ask, or you feel that you can't turn to them for information or support, try to think of other people who could help.

Grandparents

Don't assume that because your grandparents are of an older generation they won't have up-to-date ideas and information. They often do. You may also find that they have more time, and sometimes more patience, to sit and talk to you and to listen to your thoughts and concerns. Some young people really enjoy hearing the stories of their grandparents' youth and how times have changed. It may also be fun hearing from a grandparent what they remember about your parent's childhood and adolescence.

Other adults

You may have a close enough relationship with one of your aunts, uncles or perhaps a close family friend to be able to talk with them about growing up.

If you do choose to talk about personal matters with someone other than a parent, you will need to understand that this person may feel obliged to tell your parents, particularly if he/she has some concerns about what you say. You might like to discuss this with the person first and hear his/her opinion, especially if you want the subject to be confidential.

Adults other than your parents may have different opinions from your parents; it is important to consider different points of view before you make a decision. Keep in mind that while you are young, you are under the care of your parents, and that they are responsible for you. This means that you should respect your parents' ideas and decisions rather than those of another adult. For example, if your parents believe that you are too young to go out with someone on your own, even if another adult says differently, you really should follow your parents' wishes. Of course, you still have the option of trying to negotiate with your parents to try to get them to reconsider or come to a compromise.

Brothers, sisters and friends

Brothers, sisters and friends are often a good source of information. They may be happy to share their experiences and to answer your questions. Just remember, though, that the information they have may not be correct and their experiences will be different from yours.

Teachers or school counsellors

Many schools teach about sexuality as a part of human relationships or health education. This subject gives you the opportunity to learn factual information and discuss particular issues at school. Many teachers encourage their students to ask questions about anything that they don't understand.

Even if sexuality is not taught at your school, you can still approach teachers for help with information or advice. This may not necessarily be your class teacher. It might be a teacher that you have had in a previous year, or one you have come to know and trust. Some schools have counsellors, guidance officers or a nurse. You usually need to make an appointment to see them.

Community organisations

Sometimes people feel alone, with no one to turn to. If ever there is a time when you feel this way and you need someone to talk to or some help or advice, you can phone a number of community agencies. You can find many of these online. They vary from town to town, but usually include a help line for young people.

The internet

There are some great websites that have information about puberty and growing up. However, you need to be cautious about what you read online, as the information is not always correct.

When you are using the internet to get information about sex you may accidentally come across things that are disturbing. These sites may present sexuality in a negative and violent way, and may show things that are illegal. If you do come across any sites that make you feel uncomfortable or worried, tell your parent or carer.

Books

There are lots of books about growing up and sexuality. Some are just for girls or boys, some deal with specific issues and others are more general. You can find these in your school library or your local public library as well as in bookstores.

There are also magazines that cover some of the issues discussed in this book. These are generally targeted towards teenage girls but they are often read by boys as well.

If you are confused or concerned about anything you read, whether in a book, magazine or online, talk to someone you trust.

Important note to readers

Although every effort has been made to ensure that the contents of this book are accurate, it must not be treated as a substitute for medical consultation. Always consult a qualified medical practitioner. Neither the authors nor the publisher can be held responsible for any loss or claim arising out of the use, or misuse, of the suggestions made or the failure to take advice.

Index